THE
Nouvelle
YENTA
COOKBOOK
Farewell to Heartburn Hotel

THE
Nouvelle
YENTA
COOKBOOK
Farewell to Heartburn Hotel

JEANNIE SAKOL

BARRICADE BOOKS
New Jersey

Published by Barricade Books Inc., 1530 Palisade Avenue, Fort Lee, NJ 07024
Distributed by Publishers Group West, 4065 Hollis, Emeryville, CA 94608

DESIGN: Stanley S. Drate/Folio Graphics Co. Inc.

Printed in the United States of America.

Sakol, Jeannie.
  The nouvelle yenta cookbook / Jeannie Sakol.
    p.   cm.
  ISBN 0-942637-48-8 (pbk.) : $12.95
  1. Cookery, Jewish.   I. Title.
TX724.S24   1992
641.5′676—dc20   91-40777
                                                    CIP

For Henry Sakol
the "Matzo Brie King"
and in loving memory of
Rose Sakol and Fan Abrahams
who gave me "extra helpings"
of life's goodness.

Special thanks to: "Aunt Beanie" Tenenbaum,
Phyllis Canner, Ruth Bodker, Madeleine Amgott,
Lynda Gilman, Minna Saxe, Eve Arnold,
Rose Tobias Shaw, Adelle Sardi,
Juliette Mcginniss-Nelson, Jackie Reinach,
Miriam Sakol, Jerome Minkow,
Paul and Ruth Nathan, Toby Faber, Leonard Peters,
Carol Atkinson

And to Lyle and Carole Stuart, the publisher and
editor who knew what they wanted—and got me to
do it!

Contents

About the Nouvelle Yenta

◆

The term *yenta* has been for generations a mark of derision bordering on contempt. As Leo Rosten explained in *The Joys of Yiddish*, a yenta was once a woman of low origin or vulgar manners; a shrew; a shallow, coarse termagent; a gossip and rumor monger. Gradually this characterization expanded to mean an opinionated know-it-all. The yenta became the self-appointed arbiter of almost every aspect of life from family relationships, clothes and decor to sex, money, marriage, children and—most especially—food.

More recently, the yenta has evolved into a term of ferocious respect (albeit with a soupçon of fear) along with a kind of messianic pride among the nouvelle yentas themselves.

What was once perjorative is now affectionate.

You needn't be Jewish or kosher or female to be a credit card carrying nouvelle yenta who manages to combine the honored traditions of the ages with the contemporary concerns of health. Like some of the following *Nouvelle Yenta* recipes, the nouvelle yenta is a little of this, a little of that.

Wise, resourceful, imaginative and energetic, the nouvelle yenta knows what's best and generously shares that knowledge and conviction. From being an enforcer, the yenta has evolved into a re-enforcer of traditions, values and knowledge born of experience.

The nouvelle yenta still comes on strong and will not suffer fools or challenge. As my Aunt Fanny used to say, "Pay attention. You could learn something."

And meantime, have a little something to eat.

—Jeannie Sakol
New York, 1992

Farewell to Heartburn Hotel

◆

Back in the Pre-Cholesterol Era before the advent of low-fat, sodium-free and substitute everything, the rich, greasy old-time yenta dishes may have nearly destroyed the body but they did nourish the soul. Butter, chicken fat, salt, heavy cream and multiple egg yolks were central to what made yenta cooking so tasty and satisfying.

It put meat on skinny little bones. It gave meaning to family and religious occasions. It produced a Proustian remembrance of things past and a shared nostalgia for dishes that expressed their time and place in the immigrant past of most Jewish Americans.

Today chicken fat is for the most part a fond if fragrant memory, salt a shameful habit, cream and egg yolks a guilty aberration that may require counseling and sugar a brutal affront to body, brain and teeth.

We can look back in hunger at the following recipes. We can try them and probably discover they really are too rich, too heavy and altogether "too much" for our nouvelle taste buds to appreciate. At the very least, we can smile and give thanks for the memories.

Cholent

◆

In the kosher tradition of Orthodox Jews, lighting a fire and therefore cooking was forbidden between the Sabbath period of sunset Friday and sunset Saturday. Cholent evolved as a hearty dish that could be partially cooked and then left in a low oven just before Friday sunset and allowed to slowly cook for 24 hours. The lengthy simmering of meat, beans, and potatoes created a hearty, flavorful one-pot meal.

> 1 pound dried large lima beans
> 3 large yellow onions, diced
> 3 tablespoons chicken fat
> 3 pounds beef brisket
> 2 cloves garlic, crushed
> 1 pound white potatoes, peeled and quartered
> 3 tablespoons flour
> Salt, pepper, paprika
> Boiling water

Soak the lima beans overnight or use canned lima beans instead (drain and rinse off the can liquid). In a large heavy pot, sauté the onions in hot chicken fat until brown. Take out the onions and set aside. Rub the meat with garlic. Season with salt, pepper, and paprika and brown on all sides in the hot oniony fat. Put back the onions. Add the lima beans and potatoes. Sprinkle with the flour. Add boiling water to cover. Bring to a boil. Cover tightly and bake in a 450° oven for half an hour. Add a little more boiling water if necessary. Turn the oven down to 250° and allow to simmer overnight.

The result has been described by some as ecstasy, stick-to-your-ribs delicious, and cement.

Stuffed Kishke

(also called Stuffed Derma or Helzel)

◆

Still a nostalgic staple at weddings and celebrations of bar and bat mitzvahs, the kishke itself is either a beef casing from a kosher butcher or the neck skin of a large turkey also from a knowledgeable butcher but one which you can prepare yourself.

Wash beef casings in cold water; scrape clean; rinse with warm water inside and out. Cut the casing into manageable 10-inch lengths. Sew up one end of each in order to stuff them from the other. Turkey neck skin must also be thoroughly washed and then sewn in open-ended "socks" for stuffing.

STUFFING
1 cup *sifted flour*
½ cup *matzo meal*
¼ cup *grated onion*
1¼ *teaspoon salt*
¼ *teaspoon pepper*
1 *teaspoon paprika*
1 cup *chicken fat*

Blend flour, matzo meal, grated onion, seasonings, and ¾ cup of the chicken fat. Stuff the casings and sew up the open ends. Boil in salted water for one hour. Put the remaining ¼ cup chicken fat and the sliced onions in a roasting pan with the stuffed kishke on top and roast in a 350° oven 1½ hours, basting often, or roast the kishke in the same pan as the meat or poultry on the menu. Serve kishke warm, not hot; it will slice more easily. If you've made too much stuffing, pan-fry the leftovers with gravy.

Chicken Fat and Griebeners

◆

Cut away the pale yellow clumps of fat from every part of the chicken. Remove the fatty skin. Cut it all into small pieces and cook in a heavy frying pan over very low heat until the fat is completely rendered into liquid and the bits of skin have turned crisp and crackling. A clove of garlic and a chopped onion are optional during the slow rendering.

Allow to cool. Pour through a strainer to separate the liquid chicken fat from the griebeners. Store the chicken fat in a glass jar in the refrigerator for cooked recipes or for spreading on matzos or bread or serving with chopped liver.

Griebeners are like the crisp cracklings of other roasts—beef, pork, duck, and goat, but poetically better—and are traditionally served on top of mashed potatoes or with the chicken fat on matzos or bread.

THAT'S CHUTZPAH!

When you ask your hostess if you can bring something and she says just bring yourself and that's what you bring—that's chutzpah!

Real Mashed Potatoes

◆

6 good-sized baking potatoes
2 teaspoons salt
½ cup sweet butter
1 cup sweet cream
1 clove of garlic
1 bay leaf
Griebeners
Chicken fat

Peel and quarter potatoes. Place in a large pot of cold water with cut garlic clove, bay leaf, salt. Bring to a boil. Cover and cook until tender, about 25 minutes. Drain. Discard the garlic and bay leaf. Return potatoes to the hot pot and shake for a few minutes to dry.

In a large bowl, mash potatoes with an old-fashioned potato masher or a large wooden spoon. Gradually add the sweet butter and cream, mashing until they are thoroughly absorbed and the potatoes are whipped smooth.

Serve at once with a puddle of chicken fat and griebeners on top.

To keep warm, put the mashed potatoes in a heat-proof bowl and place that in a larger pan of hot water.

Serves 4–6.

Potato Kugel

◆

2 small onions
1 egg
1 teaspoon matzo meal
2 medium potatoes, scrubbed but not peeled
Chicken fat
Griebeners

In food blender put egg and onions and blend. Cut potatoes and add to the liquified onions, being careful not to over-blend; leave coarse. Spread chicken fat and griebeners on top and bake in a pie pan at 350° for an hour or until brown. If the mixture is not to be cooked at once, put in refrigerator to keep from darkening. You can make two or three batches for large numbers. Do not put more than ¾-inch thickness in a pie pan, as they taste better crisp and thin.

CHERISHED
HAND-ME-DOWNS

Like the embroidered lace shawl that once graced great grandma's parlor table, or the garnet lavaliere shaped like a peacock, or the cut crystal candy dish now consigned to holding carrot sticks, there are certain precious and personal recipes that are passed along with tender loving care.

Each of the following hand-me-downs brings with it the additional invisible ingredient of the genesis of the dish and a glimpse into the private life of the cook.

I Remember Marcia

◆

For world famous photojournalist Eve Arnold, food and friendship are interrelated. Philadelphia born and a member of the prestigious Magnum Photo Agency, she has lived in London for several years, offering warm hospitality to visitors ranging from John Huston, Isabella Rossellini, and Misha Baryshnikov to such jet-lagging unknowns as me. Her menus encompass her Jewish roots as well as dishes reflecting her years in Britain, her travels to Russia, China, India, the Middle East, and throughout the United States.

Yet, true to her generous spirit, her contribution to this book is not a celebrity dish or even a recipe she herself originated. Rather she credits "my beloved friend, Marcia Panama, sadly now gone. It was very popular among our expatriate friends in London in the sixties and early seventies. Not only is it delicious but it can be prepared in advance."

Marcia's Moroccan Chicken—Now adopted by Eve

◆

Slice whole lemons into thin slices (12) and knock out seeds. Put into colander with coarse salt to drain. Discard liquid. Pack lemon slices, with whatever salt clings to lemons, in crock or covered jar. Fill with olive oil. Let stand until bubbles come to the top (usually 3 or 4 days). Then—

2½- or 3-pound chicken—cut into 8 serving pieces
½ cup olive oil
Teaspoon salt & pepper
1 large onion, chopped
¾ can (16 oz.) tomatoes, drained and chopped
2 cloves crushed garlic
1 teaspoon sugar
1 teaspoon each ground ginger, coriander, and cumin
2 pinches saffron
½ teaspoon pepper
12 green pitted olives
12 slices preserved lemons (from first part of recipe)
1½ cups chicken broth
¼ cup blanched sliced almonds
¼ cup currants

Sauté chicken in olive oil until brown on both sides. Put in warm platter, with salt and pepper. Sauté onions till translucent. Add tomatoes, garlic, all seasonings, lemons, and broth, and mix.

Put chicken back in pan and spoon sauce over (leave lemons in sauce). Simmer gently 20 minutes. Add currants and almonds. Cover tightly with aluminum foil pierced with several holes. Bake 40 minutes in oven or till tender.

Serve with rice or burgul (bulgur wheat).

Serves 4.

Note: If in a hurry to soften lemons, freeze the lemons (after salting and putting in oil) in the freezer for a couple of hours. After freezing they will be the right texture.

Minna's Roast Chicken With Apple Stuffing

◆

2 3-pound chickens
2 teaspoons dried sage
2 teaspoons dried marjoram
1 teaspoon garlic powder
1 teaspoon salt
¼ teaspoon pepper
3 tablespoons oil

FOR STUFFING:
2 medium-size onions
1½ cups slice celery
3 large apples
¼ cup chicken fat or oil
2 tablespoons fresh chopped parsley
2 teaspoons dried sage
½ teaspoon salt
¼ teaspoon pepper
3 cups crumbled matzos
1½ cups apple juice

Chop onions and sauté with sliced celery in chicken fat or oil until tender. Peel and core apples and chop small. Combine with parsley, sage, salt, and pepper and stir into onions and celery. Add crumbled matzos. Stir. Add apple juice. Toss gently. Refrigerate mixture until ready to stuff chickens.

To prepare chickens, rinse and pat dry. Just before cooking, stuff body cavities lightly with apple stuffing. Tie drumsticks securely to the tail. Tie wings to the breasts or twist under the backs. Place both chickens side by side, breast side up, on a rack in a shallow roasting pan.

Crush sage, rosemary, and marjoram and combine with garlic powder, salt, pepper, and oil. Brush mixture over chickens. Roast uncovered in a 375° oven about 1½ hours or until drumsticks move easily. When the chickens are done, remove from oven and cover with foil to keep warm. Let stand 15 minutes before carving.

If you've made too much stuffing mixture, bake what's left in a covered casserole in a 375° oven 30 minutes.

Kathy's Grandmother's Bilkess

◆

When Katharine Karr-Kaitin was a little girl known as Kathy, her Grandmother Rose won her heart with a special dish called bilkess. Now a mother herself, Kathy has put her own mother on notice to make bilkess for her infant grandson as soon as he's old enough to eat it.

2 onions, chopped
½ pound chicken livers, cut up small
5 medium potatoes
1 egg, hard cooked in advance
Sour cream (optional)

Peel and boil the potatoes. Sauté onions with chicken livers in chicken fat or butter. Season with salt and pepper. Mash potatoes with the white of the hard-cooked egg or with enough sour cream to make a thick dough. (Save egg yolk for something else.) Dampen hands and put a spoonful of liver mixture on a pat of potatoes large enough to enfold it into a turnover shape. Bake on a cookie sheet at medium heat until brown. Serves three children, two adults.

Note: ½ pound of hamburger meat may be substituted for the chicken livers.

Grandma Rosie's Marvelous Mondlebrot

◆

Being a light sleeper, Grandma Rosie did a lot of her baking in the middle of the night when Henry was asleep, the house was quiet, and she could lose herself in the pleasures of the kitchen. Known for her stuffed cabbage, stuffed veal, and such old-fashioned cold buffet dishes as Seven Layer Party Loaf (the kind "frosted" with cream cheese), her most sought-after triumph was her Marvelous Mandebrot. Children, grandchildren, friends, and relatives and *their* children clamored *not* so much for the recipe but for the final product made with her own loving hands and packed in wax-paper-lined cookie tins for her nearest and dearest.

Like so many fondly recalled "Proustian" recipes, this one is written in her own hand. Since Grandma was incapable of deception, we can be sure nothing is left out except her talent. Her daughter Phyllis carries on the mondlebrot tradition with equally marvelous results and a waiting list of friends and relations. Her one change in the recipe is safflower or canola oil in place of butter or corn oil.

THAT'S CHUTZPAH!

Dinner party guest who brings small children without checking first. (Variation . . . guest who bring their pooch without asking.)

Rose's Marvelous Mondlebrot

◆

3 eggs, beaten
1 cup oil (safflower/canola)
2 teaspoons vanilla extract
1 cup sugar
1 cup raisins
1 cup chopped walnuts
3 to 3½ cups flour with
1 teaspoon baking powder combined with
Pinch salt

1. Beat eggs.
2. Add sugar and vanilla and beat again.
3. Add oil and beat again.
4. Add raisins and nuts, mix well.
5. Mix flour, baking powder, and salt separately.
6. Add dry ingredients to sugar mixture—mixing until nuts and raisins are equally mixed and the flour is not visible.
7. Divide mixture in half. Shape each half into a long strip on a lightly oiled cookie sheet. Moisten hands with cold water to help shape strips. It is best to place each strip on the side of the cookie sheet.

Bake in slow oven 325° to 350° for about ¾ hour or until golden in color.

Remove from oven. Let cool enough to cut with sharp knife. Make 1 inch slices, turning slices on side.

Rearrange slices around cookie sheet and bake another 15 minutes.

This final step really adds to the flavor of the mondlebrot. You can even toast the cookies 15 minutes on each side for that extra special touch.

Let cool. Stores very well in tin cookie can.

Cousin Becky's Cold Beet Borscht

◆

4 large beets
1 large onion, peeled and chopped
4 cups water, boiled
1 tablespoon salt
¼ cup fresh lemon juice
3 tablespoons sugar
1 pint sour cream

OPTIONAL:
Boiled potato
Diced cucumber
Dill

Scrub beets thoroughly. Cover with cold water and boil 15 minutes or until tender enough to pierce with a toothpick. Reserve the liquid in a bowl. Pull the skins off the beets and chop fine. Add chopped onion. Add beets and onion to reserved liquid. Stir and pour into large pot of boiling water. Add salt. Reduce heat and cook for 5 minutes. Add lemon juice and sugar. Cool and pour into glass jars to chill in the refrigerator. Serve 6 in a soup bowl or eight in a tall glass. In a soup bowl, add a boiled potato, a tablespoon of diced cucumber a heaping tablespoon of sour cream and a sprinkling of dill, preferably fresh.

In a tall glass, omit the potato (it's too cumbersome), stir in a teaspoon diced cucumber, sour cream to taste and sprinkling of dill.

Aunt Fan's No-Fooling-Around Quick Hot Borscht

◆

Aunt Fan didn't believe in complicated recipes or precise measurements. To her, starvation was imminent, a dark specter hanging over every member of the family. Her mission in life was to feed our faces. When we couldn't eat another mouthful and were begging for mercy, she would give us a jar to take home.

1 pound cabbage, shredded or coarsely chopped
Piece of middle chuck (about 1 pound)
Marrow bone or breastbone
4½ glasses of water
½ glass tomato juice
Lemon
Sugar or sugar substitute

Put everything in pot. Cover. Cook about 2 hours. Remove bone from pot. Remove meat and cut into serving sized pieces. Put back into pot. Add lemon juice and sugar to taste.

Aunt Elaine's Kasha Varnishkes

◆

Kasha is another name for old-fashioned buckwheat groats. Served with bowtie-shaped pasta it makes a simple and satisfying one-dish meal.

Kasha *(Buckwheat Groats)*
1 egg
1 cup kasha *(whole roasted buckwheat groats)*
2 cups chicken broth
2 tablespoons butter or margarine

Beat the egg lightly in a bowl; stir in kasha and salt to taste. Toast the kasha in a non-stick or heavy cast iron frying pan until the grains give off a nutty fragrance.

Bring the chicken broth to the boil in a lidded saucepan. Slowly stir in the toasted kasha and add the fat. Cover the saucepan tightly and cook about 20 minutes. Stirred with a fork, the grains should be dry and separate, ready to serve. Use in the recipe below; if necessary reheat kasha in 125° oven.

Kasha Varnishkes
1 cup diced yellow onions
1 tablespoon butter or margarine
1 teaspoon vegetable oil
1 cup of bowtie egg noodles
2 cups cooked kasha, prepared from 1 cup of raw buckwheat
groats as in the recipe above.

Sauté the onions in butter and oil until translucent but not brown. Meanwhile boil the bowtie noodles in large pot of water, salted according to taste, for 10 minutes. Combine the noodles, kasha and onions, and serve.

Lynda's Not-Just-for-Passover Coconut Macaroons

◆

Seattle-based filmmaker Lynda Gilman originally found this recipe in an old cookbook and has baked it so many times she can reel off the ingredients and method by heart.

4 egg whites
¼ cup cold water
⅔ cup sugar
¼ teaspoon salt
1 tablespoon flour
2½ cups shredded coconut

Beat eggs whites with water until stiff. Add sugar gradually, while still beating, until combined. Blend in salt and flour carefully. Fold in coconut. Stir gently. Drop mixture from a teaspoon on cookie tin lined with heavy parchment paper. Bake 25 to 30 minutes at 350°. Makes about 30 macaroons.

Cousin Florrie's Four-Layer Frosted Sandwich Loaf

◆

1 large unsliced white bread loaf (a day or two old)
1 cup each of 3 different fillings (tuna salad, egg salad, ham salad)
1 small jar chopped pimiento
1 small jar each of pitted black and green olives
Mayonnaise
2 8-ounce packages cream cheese
Milk

Chill the bread for a while for easier handling. Using a sharp knife, cut off all the crust, leaving an oblong block of bread. Carefully cut the bread in half horizontally into 2 thick even layers. Cut each of these horizontally so you have 2 more layers. Start with the bottom layer. Cover it with a thin coating of mayonnaise and spread the tuna salad evenly. Top with the second layer of bread, repeat the thin coating of mayonnaise, and spread the egg salad evenly. Top with the third layer of bread; repeat the mayonnaise coating and spread the ham salad evenly. Top with the fourth layer of bread.

Soften the cream cheese with a little milk until it has the consistency of cake frosting. Cover the entire sandwich loaf with the cream cheese mix and chill for at least 2 hours. Just before serving, garnish with sliced or chopped black and green olives and red pimiento strips in a festive design.

For variation: Use walnuts, red caviar or sprigs of watercress.

To serve: Cut slices as you would from a cake loaf, about a half inch thick, and serve on plates with forks. (It would be too messy to eat with the fingers.)

Kindly Uncle Roger's Salami and Eggs

◆

Roger Price grew up in a coal town in West Virginia where his father was a mining engineer. He was educated at a strict military academy and did not discover kosher salami until he was fully grown and living in New York. His way of dishing up salami and eggs was not too different from the norm, but whenever I think of it (and occasionally make it) I think of him.

> *Kosher salami (really garlicky, unsliced)*
> *Eggs (two per serving)*
> *Salt and pepper*
> *Chicken fat or butter*

The reason for using unsliced salami is that pre-sliced packaged salami tends to be too dry.

Be sure to remove any outer plastic wrap from salami before cutting into ¼ inch slices, 4 small or 2 large slices per serving. Put a small amount of fat or butter in a heavy skillet. Fry the salami slices over a low heat until they begin to curl up; turn them over. Frying a few minutes on each side makes them juicy and slightly crusty.

Meantime, beat up the eggs with a touch of salt and pepper. Pour over the salami and let set to let the bottom brown. Test and loosen from the pan with a spatula until the mixture is firm enough to turn over and brown the other side.

This is Roger's recipe, of course, and he liked chicken fat and butter and plenty of salt and pepper. Since kosher salami is both spicy and greasy, this recipe works well without fat or additional seasonings.

Jeannie's Makes-Men-Pay-Attention Heart-Shaped Meat Loaf

◆

2 pounds of ground chuck steak
1 slice white bread with crusts cut off
1 large onion chopped very fine
1 clump of fresh parsley, chopped very fine
1 big glob of tomato soup right out of the can, not diluted (about ½ cup)
1 big glob of sour cream (about ½ cup)
2 cloves garlic (crushed in garlic press; no garlic powder!)
1 egg
Salt
Pepper
Paprika

Dump the meat in Grandma's wooden chopping bowl. Wet the slice of white bread with water. Mush it through the meat. Throw in all the rest of the ingredients. Mush it all together with your hands (nobody's looking!). Add salt and pepper. Form into a heart shape on a baking pan.

An hour before you want to serve, preheat the oven to 350°. Slide the meat loaf in. About a half hour later, pour the rest of the can of tomato soup over the top and sprinkle some paprika on. Set the timer for ½ hour, cooking one hour altogether.

Slide the meat loaf onto a big silver tray. Ring it with fluffy mashed potatoes (real potatoes, not the packaged kind!). Serve with tangy fresh spinach-and-mushroom salad. Serves 2 for an entire romantic weekend.

Jackie Reinach's Zuppa Di Tutti

(Jewish Minestrone)

◆

A great winter Sunday night one-dish party!

Note: This is essentially a rich chicken soup with minestrone ingredients added to make a country dinner in a bowl.

STEP ONE: THE CHICKEN SOUP (Do this ahead and freeze, or the day before serving)

Make a chicken broth with a stewing chicken, leeks, onions, carrots, celery.* Cook until all the flavor is in the broth and the chicken has had it. About an hour. Cool. Strain. Defat by leaving the pot overnight in refrigerator and skimming before freezing.

*Cover with water in a *large* (8–10 quart) pot.

STEP TWO: THE CHICKEN FOR THE ZUPPA

Either serving day, or the day before, cook a *new chicken* in the chicken broth from Step One. Cook a large (5–6 pound) roasting chicken just until the meat is tender. This will take 1 to 2 hours, depending on size of bird. Remove. Cool. Take all meat off bones and cut into chunks. This step can also be done ahead of time, freezing the meat and refreezing the stock. Makes at least 2 quarts.

STEP THREE: THE VEGETABLES PLUS

(Approximate amounts for 2 quarts broth for 8 hearty servings)

½ cup olive oil

3 tablespoons butter

1 cup thinly sliced yellow onion

Garlic (3–6 cloves depending on your taste)

1 cup diced carrots

1 cup diced celery

2 cups peeled, diced potatoes
1 yam, diced
1 turnip, sliced
1½ cups cooked white beans (canned or dried and soaked/cooked)
2 cups diced zucchini (about 2 medium)
1 cup ditali or elbow macaroni
1 cup diced green beans
3 cups shredded white cabbage (savoy)
⅔ cups canned Italian tomatoes with their juice

Choose a soup pot large enough to hold everything. Put in the oil, butter, and sliced onion and garlic and cook over medium low heat until the onion wilts. Add carrots and cook for 2 to 3 minutes.

Repeat this procedure with the celery, potatoes, yam, green beans, and turnip. Then add the shredded cabbage and stir for a few minutes.

Add 2 quarts chicken broth and tomatoes. Cover and simmer over low flame about two hours, or until vegetables are tender but not mushy.

YOU CAN COOK TO THIS POINT A DAY AHEAD.

About 20 minutes before serving, add:
The chunked chicken meat (brought to room temperature)
Ditali or elbow macaroni
Zucchini
plus (optional)
Tortellini (bought from Italian markets and preferably filled with
    pesto)

When macaroni and tortellini are done, stir in about ¾ cup of your favorite pesto (garlic, basil, pine nuts, cheese). Which you can make or buy. Serve with grated parmesan cheese on the side to sprinkle on top.

It's a lot of trouble, but it's terrific as a one-dish dinner for a crowd.

Also, add or subtract vegetables at will. The cabbage really seems to be important, though, for texture.

Aunt Thelma's Carrot Ring

◆

1 cup Crisco
¾ cup brown sugar
1 cup grated carrots (firmly packed)
1 teaspoon cinnamon
½ teaspoon nutmeg
2 eggs separated
Juice of ½ lemon and rind
1¼ cup cake flour
½ teaspoon baking soda
1 teaspoon baking powder

Cream shortening and sugar. Add carrots. Beat egg yolks separately until they are thick and lemony. Add to mix. Sift flour and spices together and add to mixture. Beat egg white stiffly and fold in.

Pour batter into a greased 6-cup ring mold. Bake at 350° for 45 minutes, or until a knife inserted comes out clean. Run a knife around the mold to loosen. Invert over a plate and unmold.

THAT'S CHUTZPAH!

Dinner party host who allows pets to frolic on guests and food. ("Muffs is one of the family!")

Jackie Reinach's "Original" Pink Potato Salad

◆

Cook red potatoes whole in their skins. Slice while warm. Cook beets in microwave as per instructions for your oven. (Wrap large beets individually in plastic.) Cut beets into chunks. Use about ⅓ as many beets as potatoes.

Mix sliced potatoes and beets with scallions, sliced, white and green parts (about 1 bunch scallions to 1 dozen small potatoes).

Mix non-fat plain yogurt with Coleman's mustard to taste (more or less spicy, depending on your palate). Add 1 to 2 tablespoons sweet relish. Salt and pepper to taste. Combine with potato-beet mixture.

Salt to taste. You can add chopped parsley, chopped green pepper, radishes, as desired.

Paul Nathan's Ragged Potato Pancakes

◆

My mother's parents came to San Francisco from Germany, and I assume this recipe came with them. The ingredients, for a main course for two:

> 4 good-sized potatoes
> 2 onions
> 2 eggs
> Matzo meal or all-purpose white flour

Peel potatoes. Dry with dish towel or paper towels. Grate them. This may be done with a food processor or, preferably, by hand, using medium holes on grater. The hand method results in irregularity and a less homogenized texture, also giving a ragged, shaggy look to the edges. Stir potatoes and onions in a bowl with eggs and as much matzo meal or flour as required to create enough body to hold pancake shape when the mixture is spooned onto a hot frying pan. The pan should have been thinly coated with vegetable or light olive oil. Do not make pancakes too thick or insides will not get done. Cook at medium high heat, turning pancakes as they brown. More oil may be added as needed.

For persons accustomed to a low-salt diet, salt from the onions may be sufficient. For those used to more salt, a pinch or two can be mixed in or added upon serving.

Dry cooked pancakes between paper towels to remove excess oil. Then place on sheet in oven turned to moderate heat. This will keep one set warm and finish cooking them through while next set is in frying pan.

The traditional, delicious accompaniment to potato pancakes is apple sauce.

Toby Faber's Stuffed Cabbage

◆

1 large head cabbage
3 pounds chopped beef
3 eggs
½ cup rice (optional)
Grated onion, small
Salt
2 or 3 onions
3 8-ounce cans tomato sauce
3 lemons, sliced
1 cup sugar
½ cups white raisins

Place large cabbage in boiling water. Remove and separate leaves, placing them in colander to drain. Reserve a few leaves for shredding. Stuff leaf with a portion of the above mixture.

In large pot place the remaining leaves of cabbage, shredded. Slice 2 or 3 onions and lay on shredded cabbage. On top of this place stuffed cabbage leaves. Add 3 cans tomato sauce, 3 sliced lemons, 1 cup sugar, and ½ cup white raisins.

Cook covered 2½ to 3 hours.

THAT'S CHUTZPAH!

Dinner party host who puts on TV during dinner.

Adelle Sardi's Marvelous Main Dish Chunky Vegetable Soup

◆

2 carrots, peeled
1 white turnip, peeled
1 rib celery, cleaned
1 piece cabbage (about 4 ounces)
2 or 3 potatoes, peeled and cut into chunks
1 zucchini, rinsed, trimmed
3 cloves garlic
4 scallions, cleaned
1 onion, peeled
1 tablespoon corn oil
2 tablespoons unsalted butter
6 cups boiling water
2 teaspoons salt
Handful fresh parsley or basil leaves, or mixture—or one teaspoon
 dried basil
6 whole peppercorns
1 bay leaf or bouquet garni bag

1. Chop, slice carrots, turnip, celery, cabbage, potatoes in sizes appropriate to ultimate eating.
2. Heat oil and butter in large stockpot.
3. Chop onion coarsely, mince garlic, chop scallions; add to heat, sauté about 3 minutes.

4. Add carrots, turnip, celery, cabbage, potatoes mixing well.
5. Add water, salt, dried basil if no fresh herbs; cover, bring to boil, reduce heat, simmer gently about 25 minutes.
6. Slice zucchini, add to pot, gently boil 4 more minutes.

Meanwhile chop alternate fresh herbs, mix into soup, turn off heat, remove cover slightly to keep colors bright. Adjust seasonings. Reheat to boil just before serving. An oven-warmed, hand-sliced, hearty whole-grain or sourdough-rye bread service is recommended. Serves 6 to 8.

Toby Faber's 2-Stage Noodle Kugel

◆

Boil ¼ pound broad noodles in salted water.
Drain and mix with ¼ pound butter
Add: ½ pint sour cream
  1 pound cottage cheese
  1 small can peaches or raisins

Mix and chill overnight in a greased 10″ × 15″ pan, covered with Saran Wrap.

NEXT DAY
Beat 3 eggs and add:
½ cup sugar
2 cups milk
1 teaspoon vanilla

Pour over the noodles. Don't mix.
  Bake 1 and ¾ hours at 375° or until lightly brown.

Tante Miriam's Old-Fashioned Stuffed Cabbage

◆

1 head cabbage (2½ pounds)
½ teaspoon salt
¼ teaspoon sour salt
½ cup seedless raisins
1 pound chopped beef
¼ cup uncooked rice
¾ cup brown sugar
1 can tomato soup
½ cup boiling water

Boil cabbage in salted water 5 minutes. Drain. Remove 8 to 10 large outer leaves. Coarsely shred remaining cabbage into heavy kettle. Combine meat, salt and rice. Place 2 tablespoons of this mixture in each cabbage leaf. Roll up and secure with toothpicks. Place rolls on top of shredded cabbage. Sprinkle salt, brown sugar and sour salt over cabbage rolls. Add tomato soup, raisins and water. Cover to simmer 1½ hours, basting occasionally. Bake about 20 minutes after it is cooked to brown the top a little. Serves 4.

Lena's Old-Style Chicken Giblets and Meat Balls

◆

1 cup diced carrots
1 cup diced celery
1 onion, chopped
1 clove garlic, minced
Chicken giblets, cut in small pieces
2 cups boiling water
1½ pounds ground meat
1 can tomato soup

Sauté carrots, celery, onion, and garlic in a small amount of fat, seasoning to taste with salt, pepper, and paprika. Add giblets; simmer for half-hour. Add boiling water; simmer for another half-hour.

Season ground meat well (to taste); shape into small balls. Add meat balls to first mixture at the same time as you add can of tomato soup. Simmer for 30 minutes. Serve on rice.

Potato Knishes with Chicken Livers

◆

¾ cup salad oil
¾ cup cold water
Pinch of salt
2 drops of vinegar
2 cups flour
4 medium potatoes, boiled
1 large onion, chopped
½ pound chicken livers, cut small
2 tablespoons chicken fat

For knishes, mix salad oil, water, salt, sugar and vinegar. Add sifted flour.

Mash cooked potatoes well, add sautéed onion and chicken liver, add fat, and mix well. Roll out knish dough on floured board and fill with well mixed potatoes, onions, and chicken livers. Bake in greased pan in moderately hot oven 400°, until brown.

Leonard Peters' Jewish "French Toast"

◆

"**W**ith the anticipation most children await the arrival of Christmas morning and presents under the tree, I waited for the first morning of Passover and fried matzo for breakfast. After weeks of shopping for Passover food, substituting dishes and pots involving the entire family, the long anticipated morning finally arrived. I would stuff myself, and still do. Now whenever I visit my mother, she knows the best meal to prepare for me is what I have come to call Jewish French Toast. I hope you enjoy this dish as much as I clearly have for half a century."

> 1 pound matzo, quartered
> Salted water
> 4 eggs
> 2½ eggshells of water
> Matzo meal
> ½ pound butter
> 2 eggs, hardboiled and finely chopped
> 1 medium onion, finely chopped

1. Soak matzo in salted water only until softened. (If left in the water too long the matzo will crumble.) Remove the matzo from the water and pile on a plate where it will continue to soften until you are ready to coat and fry each piece.
2. In a bowl combine the eggs and water, beat lightly with a fork, adding matzo meal until it has a light batter texture.
3. Heat a cast iron or other heavy pan and melt the butter; place the dipped pieces of matzo in pan and fry on both sides. Add more butter as needed.
4. In advance, chop the hardboiled eggs and onion. Serve as a garnish or rolled in a piece of the fried matzo as a tortilla or sandwich filling.

Yield: 4 servings.

Poppyseed Cookies

◆

1 cup fine poppyseed
½ cup milk, scalded then cooled
½ cup butter
½ cup sugar
1½ cups flour
⅛ teaspoon salt
1 teaspoon baking powder
¼ teaspoon cinnamon
1 cup currants or seedless raisins

Soak poppyseed in milk. Cream the butter and sugar. Combine with the other ingredients in the order listed. Drop 1 teaspoon of mixture from tip of spoon onto greased cookie sheet. Bake for 20 minutes at 350°F, or till lightly browned at bottom. Slip under broiler for a few seconds to brown lightly on top.

Makes about 30 cookies.

THAT'S CHUTZPAH!

Dinner party guest who brings two guests without calling first.

Sesame Cookies

◆

3 eggs
1 cup sugar
½ cup oil
1 teaspoon vanilla
3 cups flour
1 teaspoon baking powder
½ teaspoon salt
Sesame seeds

Beat eggs, add sugar, oil, vanilla and mix well. Add flour, baking powder, and salt; mix first with large spoon then with hands until workable. Roll out ⅛ of dough into strip to thickness of little finger; cut off pieces about 5 inches long, shape like donut, and sprinkle with sesame seeds. Repeat for remainder of dough. Bake on greased cookie sheet at 350° for 15–20 minutes. Makes 50–60.

THAT'S CHUTZPAH!

Guest at a dinner party: "Didn't I tell you? I'm on a liquid diet."

Butter Cookies

◆

1 pound butter
2 eggs
1 cup sugar
4½ cups flour
4 teaspoons baking powder
1 teaspoon lemon extract
Pinch salt

Cream butter and sugar; add eggs one at a time and beat. Sift together and gradually add baking powder, salt, flour. Add lemon flavoring. Beat mixture until light. Roll out to half-inch thickness. Cut out shapes with cookie forms or a small glass. Bake on a greased cookie tin in 350° oven for 15 minutes.

Banana Bread

◆

1¾ cups all-purpose flour
2 teaspoons double acting baking powder
¼ teaspoon baking soda
¾ teaspoon salt
⅓ cup shortening
⅔ cup sugar
2 eggs
1 cup mashed bananas (2 or 3)
Cream cheese

Sift flour, measure and resift 3 times with baking powder, soda, and salt. Cream shortening and sugar until light and fluffy. Add eggs one at a time and beat well after each addition. Add bananas and mix. Add flour gradually and beat until smooth after adding each portion. Turn into well-greased pan 8×4×2½ and bake in moderate oven 350° for 50 minutes or until done. Cool on rack.

Wrap in foil and store in refrigerator. Slice thin and serve with a dab of softened cream cheese.

Gum Drop Cake

◆

¼ pound shortening
2 eggs (separated)
2 cups sifted flour (measure before sifting)
¼ teaspoon salt
1 cup raisins
¾ cup sugar
¾ cup milk
1 teaspoon baking powder
1 teaspoon vanilla
1 pound gum drops (no licorice), cut into small pieces

Cream shortening and sugar. Add egg yolks. Add dry ingredients and milk alternately; add vanilla and then the beaten egg whites. Add raisins and gum drops. Bake in 350° oven for about ¾ hour in spring form.

THAT'S CHUTZPAH!

Dinner party guests who bring their own food because they're on a special diet.

Old-Fashioned (not from a jar) Gefilte Fish

◆

2 pounds whitefish
2 pounds pike
2 pounds carp
4 large onions
2 quarts water
4 teaspoons salt
1 teaspoon pepper
3 eggs
½ teaspoon sugar
3 tablespoons matzo or cracker meal
3 carrots, sliced
ice water

Fillet the fish. Reserve head, skin and bones and combine with 3 onions, sliced, 2 teaspoons salt and ½ teaspoon pepper in 1 quart water. Cook rapidly while preparing fish. Grind fish with remaining 1 onion. Place in chopping bowl. Add eggs, water, sugar, meal and remaining salt and pepper. Chop until very fine (or chop in food processor). By now the fish stock is simmering.

Moisten hands. Shape mixture into oval-shaped balls; drop gently into stock. Add carrots. Simmer covered over low heat 1½ hours; remove cover for last half hour. Allow fish to cool slightly before transferring to a large glass baking dish. Strain stock; pour over fish. Arrange cooked carrot on top of fish as garnish. Chill overnight covered in the refrigerator. The fish stock will turn to jelly. Serve with horseradish. Makes 10 pieces.

LOTSA MATZOS

(all year round; not just for Passover)

Matzos have been part of my life since infancy. Instead of a teething ring, I chomped on a matzo. When I was old enough to follow my father into the kitchen on Sunday morning, it was to "help" him make the matzo brie by crumbling the matzos. Later still, I took peanut butter and jelly matzo sandwiches to school, and not just at Passover either.

I liked the flavor. I liked the crunch. I once used the edge of a matzo as a makeshift ruler in arithmetic class when I had lost my plastic one.

For years, I have collected matzo recipes from friends, relatives, magazines, and cookbooks and created some variations of my own.

The unleavened bread that sustained Moses and his people in the wilderness may not have been as neatly uniform as the matzos in today's food markets, but the basic components of flour and water remain the same. The Jews of the Exodus were clearly on to a good thing. As the saying goes, that one good thing has definitely led to many others.

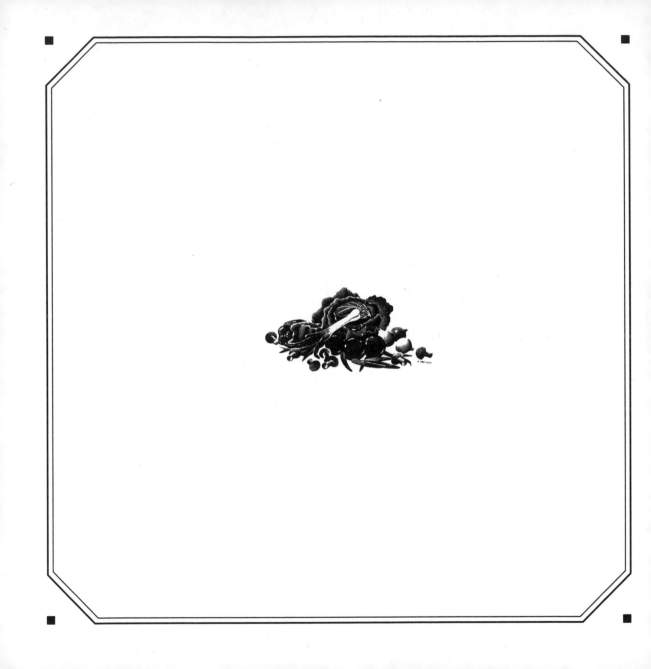

Grandpa Henry's Sunday-Morning-in-the-Bronx Matzo Brie

◆

3 matzos
2 eggs
¼ teaspoon salt
2 tablespoons butter
2 tablespoons milk
Pepper

Break matzos into smallish pieces in a bowl. Cover with water while you count to ten. Pour water off and press out the excess with a soup spoon or, better yet, your hands. Melt the butter in a frying pan. Fry the matzos until lightly toasted. Beat the eggs with milk, salt, and a dash of pepper. Pour over matzos and fry, stirring until the eggs are set. Serves 2 or maybe 3.

Madeleine Amgott's Consistently Scrumptious Matzo Balls

◆

I've had these matzo balls at Madeleine and Milton's table for over 20 years. They are always the same and always light, fluffy, and flavorful.

MATZO BALLS
2 tablespoons melted fat or oil
2 large eggs, slightly beaten
½ cup matzo meal
1 teaspoon salt, if desired
2 tablespoons soup stock or water

Blend fat or oil and eggs together. Mix matzo meal and salt together. Add matzo meal and salt mixture to egg and fat or oil mixture and blend well. Then add soup stock or water and mix till uniform. Cover mixing bowl and place in refrigerator for 15 minutes. Using a 2- or 3-quart pot bring 1½ quarts of slightly salted water to a brisk broil. Reduce heat and into the slightly boiling water drop balls about 1 inch in diameter formed from mixture from refrigerator. Cover pot and cook 30–40 minutes.

Keep soup at room temperature or warmer. Remove matzo balls from water and place in soup pot. When ready to serve, allow soup to simmer for about 5 minutes. Recipe makes about 8 matzo balls.

Jennie Grossinger's Knaidlach

◆

As a child I attended a summer camp in the Catskill Mountains in upstate New York, a matzo ball's throw from nearby Grossinger's. Occasionally, a good-natured parent would take a few of us there for a "real" meal and of course to put some meat on our skinny little bones. (I weighed in at 145 pounds at the time.)

I remember the matzo ball soup with tears in my eyes, and not because there was too much pepper. Here, from Jennie Grossinger's cookbook, are two matzo ball recipes I've tried and liked.

Jennie Grossinger's Knaidlach #1

(2 eggs and chicken fat)

◆

2 eggs
4 tablespoons melted chicken fat
⅓ cup cold water
1 teaspoon salt
1 cup matzo meal

Beat the eggs, fat, water, and salt together. Stir in the matzo meal, adding just enough to make a stiff batter. Chill 1 hour.

Form into balls and cook for 30 minutes in boiling soup or salted water. Makes about 18 matzo balls.

Jennie Grossinger's Knaidlach #2

(3 eggs; no chicken fat)

◆

3 eggs
1 teaspoon salt
¾ cup matzo meal

Separate the eggs. Beat the egg yolks and salt together. Stir in the matzo meal and chill 1 hour. Beat the egg whites until stiff but not dry and fold into the matzo meal mixture. Form into 18 balls. Cook in boiling soup or salted water for 20 minutes.

THAT'S CHUTZPAH!

Dinner party guest who answers beeper phone at the table and has a conversation. (Exceptions: doctors and the President of the United States).

Matzo Pizza

◆

The best of both worlds; it's crispy crusted and oozing with succulence.

FOR THE CRUST
2 matzos (plain or onion)
Water
2 eggs
Salt and pepper
Butter or margarine (enough to grease the pans)

FOR THE FILLING
2 medium/large zucchini
1 large onion
1 29-ounce can tomatoes (stewed, crushed or puréed)
1 8-ounce can of sliced mushrooms
Italian seasonings to taste (oregano, garlic salt or powder)

Break matzos in half or quarters. Soak in enough cold water to cover for 5 minutes. Press out as much water as possible. Add salt and pepper to eggs.

Beat eggs and pour over matzos. Arrange matzos to cover the bottom of two well-greased pie pans.

Chop zucchini and onion and combine with mushrooms, tomatoes, and seasonings. Simmer until softened. Evenly distribute the tomato mixture between the two pie pans. Sprinkle with extra oregano and parsley flakes.

Bake 30 minutes at 350° or until matzo crust browns and tomato mixture bubbles. Allow to cool slightly. Cut in pie-shaped portions. Two pies make 8 slices.

Baked Apples

◆

Large tart apples, cored but with the skin left on (1 per serving)
Equal parts matzo meal and chopped walnuts
Orange juice as needed (reckon 1 cup for 8 apples)
1 tablespoon sugar per apple
1 pitted prune per apple

Combine matzo meal and chopped walnuts with enough orange juice to
bind them together. Press mixture into cored cavity of apples, almost to
the top. Add pitted prune. Bake 30 minutes in covered baking dish at
375°. Serve warm.

Matzo Rolls

◆

3 eggs
½ teaspoon salt
¾ cup chicken broth or milk
1 cup matzo meal
⅓ cup cake meal
4 tablespoons melted chicken fat or butter

Beat together the eggs and salt. Stir in the broth (or milk) alternately with the matzo meal and cake meal. Add the melted fat or butter. Fill 12 greased muffin cups ⅔ full. Bake in a 350° oven 30 minutes or until browned.

THAT'S CHUTZPAH!

Putting everyday supermarket tea in a Fortnum & Mason tin.

Matzo Pudding

◆

2 cups grated apples
4 eggs
2 cups powdered sugar
¼ cup matzo meal
½ cup blanched almonds
½ lemon rind

Separate the eggs. Cream the sugar and beaten egg yolks. Add grated apples, lemon rind, matzo meal, and almonds. Fold in beaten egg whites. Bake in 375° oven until top is crispy, about 25 minutes. Serve with lemon yogurt. Serves 4.

Matzo Meal Nut Cake

◆

6 eggs, separated
1 cup sugar
½ cup coarse matzo meal
¼ teaspoon salt
½ teaspoon baking powder
½ pound chopped walnuts

Beat egg yolks until lemon colored. Add sugar gradually. Mix together matzo meal, baking powder, and salt and gradually beat the mixture into the egg yolks and sugar. Add chopped nuts. Fold in the well-beaten egg whites. Pour into a 9-inch-square pan. Bake in 325° oven 15 minutes and in 350° oven for another half hour. Serves 4.

Moist Matzo Stuffing

(for large turkey or two chickens)

◆

¾ cup shortening, margarine, or chicken fat
¾ cup minced onion
10 matzos, finely broken, or 7 cups matzo farfel
1 teaspoon salt
¼ teaspoon pepper
1 tablespoon paprika
1 egg
2 cans condensed chicken broth or 2 cups using bouillon cubes

Sauté onion in fat until tender but not browned. Add matzos or farfel and toast lightly. Combine seasonings, egg, and soup and add to matzo mixture. Stuff bird.

Variations:
CELERY STUFFING: Sauté 1 cup diced celery with the onion.
MUSHROOM STUFFING: Sauté 1 cup diced fresh mushrooms with the onion.
NUT STUFFING: Toast 1½ cups coarsely chopped nuts with the onion before adding matzo crumbs or farfel.
GIBLET STUFFING: Cook giblets in water until tender. Mince and add to dressing.
FRUIT STUFFING: Add 2 cups stewed prunes, drained, pitted, and chopped, plus 2 cups pared, diced apple and ½ cup raisins.

Matzo Sponge Cake

◆

⅓ cup matzo cake meal
½ cup potato starch
Pinch of salt
1 cup granulated sugar, divided
10 eggs, separated
Juice of 1 lemon (1½ tablespoons)
Grated rind of 1 orange

Sift together matzo cake meal, potato starch, and salt, 3 times; set aside. Beat egg yolks until thick. Add ½ cup sugar, lemon juice, and orange rind. Continue beating mixture until thick and fluffy. Fold in sifted dry ingredients. In separate bowl, beat egg whites until foamy; add ½ cup sugar gradually; beat until stiff peaks form. Fold egg yolk mixture into egg whites. Turn into ungreased 10-inch spring form tube pan. Bake at 350° for 45 to 50 minutes. Invert pan until cake is cool.

THAT'S CHUTZPAH!

Serving store-bought chocolate chip cookies in a David's Cookies tin.

Maxine Pinner's Matzo Farfel and Peaches

◆

1 pound matzo farfel
7 eggs, beaten
¾ pound melted margarine or butter
1 cup sugar
3 medium cans sliced peaches
2 cups peach juice
1 teaspoon vanilla
¾ teaspoon salt

Soak farfel in hot water to soften. Drain. Add eggs, fat, sugar, juice (except peach). Grease 3 quart casserole. Fill with ½ mixture, half peaches, farfel, peaches. Sprinkle with sugar and cinnamon. Bake in 350° oven for 1 hour. Serves 4.

Apple Fritters

◆

1 cup matzo meal
3 eggs, beaten
1 teaspoon salt
¾ cup water
2 medium tart apples, peeled and chopped
2 tablespoons sugar
1 teaspoon cinnamon

Combine eggs, salt, and water. Add to matzo meal. Add apples, sugar, and cinnamon; blend well. Drop by tablespoonsful into 1-inch deep hot fat and fry until golden brown. Drain on absorbent paper. Sprinkle with cinnamon and sugar. Serve with sour cream. Makes 12 to 14 fritters.

Chicken Giblet Fricassee

◆

Giblets from 2 chickens (hearts, gizzards, and necks)
3 medium onions, diced
2 matzos, finely broken
⅔ cup cold water
2 pounds ground beef
2 eggs, slightly beaten
2 teaspoons salt
¼ teaspoon pepper
2 teaspoons paprika

Cut giblets into small pieces and place in saucepan. Add diced onion and cover with water. Simmer, covered, until tender, about 1½ to 2 hours. Soak broken matzos in cold water. Combine with ground beef and beaten eggs. Shape into small meatballs and drop into hot giblet mixture. Add seasonings, cover, and simmer for at least ½ hour. Longer cooking gives a better flavor. Serves 4 to 6.

Fat-Free Matzo Balls

(could there be such a thing?)

◆

Here's a recipe I found somewhere and put in my matzo file. It's not Madeleine's or Jennie's but it is a reasonable facsimile for anyone on a fat-free diet.

> 2 eggs, separated
> ½ cup matzo meal
> Salt
> Powdered garlic
> Parsley flakes

Beat together egg yolks and a little salt. Beat whites separately until they are very stiff. Fold together and add matzo meal, powdered garlic for flavor, and a shake of parsley flakes for color. Shape into small balls. Drop immediately into vigorously boiling salted water in a large pot. Boil 45 minutes, with the pot covered.

THAT'S CHUTZPAH!

Reluctantly giving a favorite recipe—but leaving out an essential ingredient.

Matzo Meal Meatloaf

◆

1 pound each chopped beef and veal
1 medium onion, finely chopped
¼ cup horseradish
2 eggs, beaten
1 cup matzo meal
1 cup applesauce
½ cup ketchup or tomato sauce
Salt and pepper to taste

Combine all ingredients and mix well. Add more matzo meal if mixture looks too moist. Place in a loaf pan and bake in preheated 350° oven for 1 hour. Cool slightly, slice, and serve with extra horseradish or applesauce. Serves 8.

Low-Fat Matzo Brie

(low in fat but still uses eggs)

◆

2 matzos
½ cup skim milk
4 eggs, beaten
¼ teaspoon salt
Pepper
1 tablespoon *low-fat margarine*

Break matzos into small pieces into a shallow bowl; pour milk over them and stir until soft. Add beaten eggs, salt, and pepper; stir. Melt margarine in a frying pan; pour in egg mixture. Cook over low heat until bottom is lightly browned on both sides. Makes 2 servings.

Matzo Pie Crust

◆

1½ matzos
1 tablespoon fat
½ cup matzo meal
2 eggs
2 tablespoons sugar
⅛ teaspoon salt

Soak matzos in water and press as dry as possible. Heat fat in large frying pan. Add soaked matzos and cook at the lowest possible heat until matzos are firm. Transfer to large bowl. Add matzo meal, eggs, sugar, and salt. Mix well, preferably with your hands. Since this pie crust dough will not roll out, press it into your pie pan with your hands until it's evenly distributed and about ¼ inch thick.

Apple Cake

◆

8 eggs, separated
½ teaspoon salt
¾ cup sugar
8 apples, grated
1 cup matzo meal
¼ cup ground almonds
1 teaspoon cinnamon
1 tablespoon orange juice

Add salt to egg whites and beat until stiff. Add sugar gradually; beat in egg yolks. Add apples, matzo meal, almonds, cinnamon, and orange juice. Bake at 325° for 1 hour and 15 minutes, preferably in a tube pan.

THAT'S CHUTZPAH!

Dinner party guest following you into the kitchen where you're wrapping the night's leftovers in aluminum foil for tomorrow night's meal: "Oh, goody! A doggie bag for me?"

Matzo Meal Muffins

◆

2 eggs
½ teaspoon salt
1 cup water
1½ cups matzo meal
4 tablespoons chicken fat

Beat eggs with salt and water. Stir in matzo meal to make a smooth batter. Heat fat and grease muffin pans with it; stir remaining hot fat into the batter. Fill muffin pans ⅔ full with mixture and bake at 350° for 30 minutes or until brown. Serve with clear soup, roast chicken, or meat. Makes 8 large or 16 small muffins.

Variation 1: For sweet muffins, use butter in place of fat, and milk instead of water. Add sugar, cinnamon, and grated rind of lemon. Bake in the same manner.

Variation 2: Use 1 cup soaked and pitted prunes, sliced or cut fine.

Variation 3: Finely cut dates, raisins, chopped nuts, or a mixture of all three make delicious fruit muffins.

How to Make Your Own Matzo Meal

◆

Use plain whole matzos. Crush them into as small pieces as possible with your bare hands. Put them into your blender or processor set for high and dry. Mix for a few seconds and you'll have a fine powdery matzo meal. Use exactly as you would store bought meal.

LA PRUNE
DE MA TANTE

Stewed prunes? Wrinkled black globs in muddy brown juice? Yuck. Reminders of warnings in childhood of the results of impending digestive chaos. For me prunes were the "preventive" price paid for enjoying a day of hot dogs, popcorn, ice cream, sodas, and everything else "guaranteed" to upset my stomach. When cunningly added to my favorite hot cereal, oatmeal, or used as a playful garnish with my favorite tuna salad plate, prunes continued to be a trial and a terror until two things happened.

I discovered that miracle of the baker's art, the prune Danish, and my Aunt Fan introduced me to her wonders of prunes in a variety of ways including compote, sweet and sour beef stew, potato and prune tsimmes, turkey stuffing, prune whip, and stuffed prune hors d'oeuvres.

She never attempted to make a prune Danish. Certain things were better left to Zabar's, Zaro's, or comparable purveyors of "real," not packaged, baked goods. To her a prune Danish mummified by plastic wrap or supermarket freezer was beneath scorn. The rare times of weakness when I now succumb to prune Danish lust and buy either, the first bite reminds me of Aunt Fan's, "I told you so! Next time you'll listen."

Aunt Fan is no longer with us, though I feel her presence, especially when I do my best to follow her recipes and instructions.

Aunt Fan's Sweet and Sour Beef Stew

(Flumen Mit Potatoes)

◆

1. Have butcher cut up chuck (figure on about ½ pound per person) as for beef stew.
2. In large kettle place cut up meat, 1 pound prunes, 1 can tomato sauce, 1 can water, sprinkle of salt to taste.
3. When meat is partially done, add 3 or 4 carrots, potatoes sufficient for people to be served, 6 gingersnaps, pinch of clove, 3 tablespoons of honey, juice of 1 lemon or several pieces of sour sault. Taste for individual preference as to exact amount of sweet and sour.

All in one dish—just add salad and start with juice and you have a complete meal.

Brandied Prunes

(better than ordinary stewed prunes)

◆

1 pound large dried prunes
½ cup boiling water
¼ cup apricot brandy

Put prunes in a large jar with a tight-fitting lid. Add boiling water to cover all the prunes. Fasten the lid and let jar stand at room temperature for several hours or overnight. Add apricot brandy, mix thoroughly, and chill in the refrigerator until ready to serve. Delicious alone or with hot or cold cereal.

THAT'S CHUTZPAH!

Pouring house label brandy into a Courvoisier bottle and passing it off as the real imported thing.

Roast Turkey Stuffing

◆

1 pound unsweetened pitted prunes
4 cups sliced apples, skinned and cored
1 cup dry unseasoned bread crumbs
2 teaspoons lemon juice
1 tablespoon sugar
1 teaspoon cinnamon

Simmer the prunes in enough water to cover for 10 minutes. Drain. Add the apples, bread crumbs, lemon juice, sugar, and cinnamon. Mix lightly. Stuff the turkey and roast as usual.

Prune Butter

◆

2 sticks butter or margarine
1 tablespoon brown sugar
¾ cup pitted stewed prunes (from jar or can is fine)

Let butter or margarine stand at room temperature until softened. Put in mixer bowl with sugar and prunes. Beat at medium speed until blended. Cover and refrigerate. To use, let stand at room temperature for 20 minutes or so for easier spreading. Delicious on hot toast, with waffles and pancakes, and in sandwich combinations with mashed banana or as a moistener with sliced chicken, beef, or ham.

Stuffed Prunes

◆

2 dozen extra large dried prunes, soaked overnight and drained
2 cup confectioners' sugar (optional)
1 tablespoon butter
½ teaspoon vanilla
½ cup chopped walnuts

Cream butter and sugar. Add vanilla and nuts and mix until well blended. Remove pits from prunes and fill the cavities with globs of the mixture. Serve as a garnish on cold meat platters. Or roll in confectioners' sugar and serve on a dessert tray along with cookies and other sweet treats.

Crisp Apple Prune Betty

◆

4 unsalted matzos, coarsely broken
½ cup (1 stick) butter or margarine
¾ cup juice from prunes
4 teaspoons lemon juice
3 cups pared, sliced apples
1 cup pitted cooked prunes, chopped
¾ cup brown sugar, packed
1 teaspoon cinnamon

Combine matzo, fat, and juices. Combine apples, prunes, sugar, and cinnamon. In a greased 1½ quart casserole, arrange alternate layers of matzo and fruit mixtures, starting and ending with matzo mixture. Cover and bake in a moderate oven (350°) for 1 hour, uncovering during last 15 minutes. Serve warm or cold, plain, or with cream.

Potato and Prune Tzimmes

◆

1 pound prunes
1 pound brisket of beef
5 medium potatoes
Salt and pepper
½ cup sugar
1 tablespoon lemon juice

Wash and soak prunes overnight in cold water to cover. Place in kettle with meat seasoned with salt and pepper. Let cook slowly 1½ hours or until meat is nearly tender. Set aside and add potatoes (white or sweet), pared and cut in small pieces. Place meat and prunes on top, add sugar and lemon juice, cover, and place in oven until potatoes are done and all is browned. Serve hot with gravy. Serves 4.

THAT'S CHUTZPAH!

Pounding chicken breasts paper-thin and passing them off as "veal" scallopine.

Sweet Potato and Prune Tzimmes

◆

1½ pounds dried prunes
3 cups boiling water
2 tablespoons fat
3 pounds brisket
2 onions, diced
1½ teaspoons salt
¼ teaspoon pepper
3 sweet potatoes, peeled and quartered
½ cup honey
2 cloves
½ teaspoon cinnamon

Wash prunes and let soak in the boiling water ½ hour. Melt the fat in a Dutch oven. Cut the beef in 6 or 8 pieces and brown with the onions. Sprinkle with the salt and pepper. Cover and cook over low heat 1 hour. Add the undrained prunes, sweet potatoes, honey, cloves, and cinnamon. Replace cover loosely and cook over low heat 2 hours. Serves 6 to 8.

Sweet Potato and Prune Casserole (Meatless)

◆

6 medium sweet potatoes (3 pounds)
1-pound jar stewed prunes
¾ cup honey
¾ teaspoon cinnamon
1 teaspoon salt
2 tablespoons prune juice
2 tablespoons lemon juice
¼ cup melted margarine or chicken fat

Boil potatoes until tender. Skin and cut into ¼-inch slices. Cut prunes in half. Make mixture of remaining ingredients. In a 2-quart casserole, arrange alternate layers of sweet potatoes and prunes, pouring the honey mixture over each layer. Bake uncovered, basting occasionally, at 350° for 45 minutes. Serves 4.

Prune Layer Cake

◆

1 cup sugar
½ cup butter
2 eggs
¾ cup sour cream
1½ cups flour
1 teaspoon soda
2 teaspoons baking powder
1½ tablespoons cornstarch
1 cup stewed prune pulp
2 tablespoons prune juice
1 teaspoon each, cinnamon and cloves

Cream butter and sugar well together; mix dry ingredients. Combine the 2 mixtures, adding prune juice and pulp. Bake in 2 layers in a moderate oven, 350°, for 25 minutes. Spread frosting of your choice between layers and over the top. (My own favorite is chocolate fudge.)

Prunes and Beets Compote

◆

1 pound unsweetened prunes
3 cups undrained julienne beets
½ teaspoon salt
4 tablespoons sugar
2 teaspoons vinegar

Combine all the ingredients in a saucepan. Cover and cook over low heat 25 minutes or until prunes are tender. Delicious when served as an accompaniment to roast meat or poultry. Serves 4–6.

Prune Whip

◆

Sweeten 2 cups of drained, stewed prunes to taste with powdered sugar or honey. Mash through a sieve. The pulp should now be about 1½ cups. Fold in an equal quantity of whipped cream or stiffly beaten egg whites. Pile in glasses and chill. Or serve as a topping on vanilla ice cream or frozen yogurt.

THAT'S CHUTZPAH!

Passing off College Inn Chicken Broth as homemade.

Baked Prune Whip

◆

Pit 2 cups of stewed prunes, and mash to a pulp. Add 1 teaspoon of grated lemon rind, 2 teaspoons of lemon juice, and 4 tablespoons of powdered sugar. Blend well. Beat the whites of 4 eggs until stiff; add 2 tablespoons of powdered sugar and continue beating until thoroughly blended. Fold prune mixture by spoonfuls into the egg whites. Pile lightly in a greased pudding dish and bake in a moderate oven, 350°, for 30 minutes. Serve hot or cold with custard, real cream or Cool Whip, or lemon yogurt.

Prune and Matzo Farfel Tzimmes (Meatless)

◆

½ pound prunes, *washed and rinsed*
1 cup matzo farfel
3 cups boiling water
1 teaspoon salt
½ teaspoon cinnamon
Grated rind and juice of 1 lemon
½ cup honey or ¾ cup sugar
½ cup butter, oil, or vegetable shortening

Soak prunes in cold water to cover for 30 minutes. Turn prunes and liquid into cooking pot for top-of-stove cooking, or into a casserole for oven baking. Add farfel, then boiling water and the other ingredients as listed. Cook, partly covered, over moderate heat for 30 minutes. Turn into casserole and brown under broiler flame just before serving. Or, bake in covered casserole 45 minutes at 350°. Remove cover and brown under broiler flame. Should added liquid be necessary at any stage of the procedure, add boiling water—as little as necessary to prevent scorching. Serves 4.

Pickled Prune Compote

◆

Combine in a large pot, 2 cups dried prunes, 1 cup cider vinegar, 2 cups brown sugar, 1 teaspoon whole allspice, 1½ sticks cinnamon, and 1 teaspoon whole cloves with heads removed.

Simmer about 1 hour or until prunes have plumped. Remove prunes with slotted spoon and place in wide-mouth jar. Strain the cooking liquid before pouring over the prunes. Store in refrigerator. Delicious cold or warm as an accompaniment to meat or poultry.

Eggless Prune Whip

◆

½ pound dried prunes
¼ teaspoon lemon juice
2 cups water
½ cup sugar
1 tablespoon gelatin
½ cup cold prune juice
1 cup hot prune juice
Dash of salt

Stew prunes and lemon juice in water 30 minutes. Add sugar. Cook 5 minutes longer or till tender. Drain. Remove pits from prunes and put prunes through strainer. Soak gelatin in the cold prune juice and dissolve it with the hot prune juice. When mixture is cold and thickened, whip with a rotary beater till fluffy. Add salt. Fold in prune pulp and chill the mixture thoroughly. Serves 6.

THAT'S CHUTZPAH!

Guest at a dinner party: "I'm really not very hungry. I had an enormous lunch. I'll just nibble."

Prune and Apple Deep Dish Pie

◆

1 cup stewed prunes
1 cup apples, peeled and sliced
½ cup prune juice
½ cup water
⅓ cup honey
1 tablespoon fat
½ teaspoon salt
1 matzo

Drain prunes, remove pits, and cut prunes into pieces. Place alternate layers of apples and prunes in a greased baking dish. Combine the prune juice, water, fat, honey, and salt and bring the mixture to the boiling point. Pour half of this mixture over the fruit. Crumble the matzo coarsely, and let it soak in the rest of the syrup mixture until soft. Then spread the matzo and syrup mixture over the fruit. Bake in moderate oven (350°) for about 40 minutes, or until nicely browned and the apples are tender. Serves 4.

Prunes have also figured in my early education. My favorite English teacher, Catharine Jones, used a prune anecdote to illustrate the distinction between the words *and* and *with*. She told of ordering "prunes and milk" at a restaurant. When the waitress brought a dish of prunes swimming in milk, she protested, "I ordered prunes *and* milk, not prunes *with* milk."

"What's the difference?" the hapless waitress asked.

"The difference? What's the difference between a woman *and* child and a woman *with* child?"

POT ROAST, MEATLOAF—AND ONE MEATBALL

I have yet to work out a practical system for collecting recipes, especially those from friends and relatives. Ideally, I should have everything cunningly organized on file cards, cross-indexed by subject and origin with space for special notes such as when and to whom the dish has been served.

In real life, there is a kitchen drawer stuffed with clippings, supermarket handouts, scribbled envelopes, and xerox and FAX copies. On close inspection, I see that some of the older tattered recipes are actually carbon copies typed the old-fashioned way, with carbon paper.

There is also a collection of stained and battered cookbooks, their condition evidence of panic rather than wanton abuse. Tucked in their pages and straining their bindings are additional recipes of unknown origin collected for forgotten reasons.

In a gallant attempt to organize them, I discovered a preponderance of recipes for Pot Roast, Meatloaf, and Meat Balls. Gleaned from this collection are the following variations on Pot Roast and Meatloaf plus one outstanding recipe for Sweet and Sour Meat Balls.

Madeleine's Pot Roast

◆

"The secret of good pot roast is good beef, lots of onions, and garlic and slow cooking, all done the day before serving."

◆

5 onions
1 brisket of beef, 5 to 6 lbs, defatted
salt and pepper
3 cloves garlic
Parsley
Dill
2 bay leaves
8 Carrots

Slice onions thick. Add celery, parsley, garlic, bay leaves and onions as a bed for the brisket. Salt and pepper the brisket and cover with the rest of the onions in a heavy roaster with lid. Cook at 325° for at least an hour. Lay peeled whole carrots on top. (There should be no need to add water but, if too dry add one cupful of water, light stock or red wine.)

When fork tender, take the meat out, cool and slice. Remove bay leaves. When serving, put as many slices as you think you need in the juice with the veggies and add fresh dill. Heat until hot and serve on warm platter. Serves 6–8.

Toby Faber's Pot Roast

◆

Sear in a heavy dutch oven 3-pound piece of brisket of beef.
When browned add:
Large chopped onion
2 crushed cloves of garlic
Salt, pepper, paprika

Cover and simmer for 30 minutes.
Gravy will be produced by diced onion.
Add to this (if desired) a soft tomato or some canned tomatoes
    (about 3 plum tomatoes).

Simmer for 2 to 3 hours. During this period add water or some chicken broth.
When tender, cool.

Slice cooled meat against the grain. Trim fat from each slice. Pour gravy in separate bowl and place in refrigerator until cold enough to skim fat easily. Add gravy to sliced meat. Rewarm when ready to serve. Serves 6.

Old-Fashioned Pot Roast (Gedaempfte Fleisch)

◆

4 pounds brisket of beef
3 onions, diced or sliced
2 cloves garlic, minced
1 carrot, shredded
1 stalk celery, diced
1 green pepper, diced
3 tablespoons chicken fat
2 teaspoons salt
½ teaspoon paprika
4 bay leaves
10 peppercorns
1½ cups tomato juice
2 tablespoons brown sugar

Heat a heavy pot and braise the meat till evenly browned on all sides.
Add remaining ingredients in the order listed; cover and simmer 1½ to 2
hours. Slice when tender and serve with gravy from pot. Serves 6 to 8.

Manny-The-Bachelor's Pot Roast

◆

4 pounds brisket of beef
1 large onion, sliced
¼ cup chopped green pepper
½ cup chopped celery
1 11-ounce can tomato mushroom sauce
1 teaspoon salt
¼ teaspoon pepper
6 medium potatoes, peeled

Brown meat in a Dutch oven. If meat is very lean, use a little fat for browning. Add sliced onion, green pepper and celery; sauté until tender. Add tomato and mushroom sauce, salt, and pepper. Cover and simmer 2½ to 3 hours or until tender. Cut potatoes in half and add during last half hour of cooking. If desired, this may be roasted in a moderate oven (350°F) for the same length of time. Serves 6 to 8.

Sunday Night Pot Roast

◆

2½ pounds of beef (chuck, rump, or flank steak)
Salt and pepper
1 tablespoon flour
2 tablespoons fat
1 onion, chopped fine
1 cup boiling water
1 or 2 bay leaves
1 medium carrot, diced
1 sliced celery stalk
Tomato

Season meat as desired and sprinkle with flour. Heat the fat and fry the onion in it until light brown; add the meat, brown on all sides to keep in the juices. Add carrot and celery. Pour on the boiling water, add bay leaves, and cover tightly; then let simmer slowly about 2½ hours, or until tender. Add a little boiling water to prevent burning. Sliced or stewed tomato laid on top of the meat ½ hour before serving makes a fine flavor. Thicken gravy with 1 tablespoon flour.

Meat Loaf
(corn flakes variation)

◆

1 pound ground beef
1 can vegetable soup
1 egg
1 cup corn flakes
1 small grated onion
1 pinch salt and pepper

Mix meat with vegetable soup, corn flakes, onion, and egg and place in a greased pan. Bake at 350° for 35 to 40 minutes. Serves 4.

THAT'S CHUTZPAH!

Serving decaf instant coffee in a sterling silver coffee pot.

Sweet and Sour Meat Loaf

(matzo variation)

◆

2 pounds ground beef
1 medium onion
1 cup crushed matzos
¾ teaspoon salt
⅛ teaspoon pepper
½ cup water
2 eggs, beaten
1 11-ounce can tomato and mushroom sauce
¼ cup lemon juice
½ cup sugar

Combine and mix well the meat, onion, matzo crumbs, salt, pepper, water, eggs and ½ cup of the tomato and mushroom sauce. In a greased baking dish, shape into a loaf. Combine remaining tomato and mushroom sauce, lemon juice, and sugar. Pour over meat. Bake in moderate oven (350°F) 1 hour, basting frequently. Serves 6.

Meat Loaf

(applesauce variation)

◆

1 pound each ground beef and veal
1 medium onion, finely chopped
¼ cup horseradish
2 eggs, beaten
1 cup matzo meal
1 cup applesauce
½ cup ketchup
Salt and pepper to taste

Combine all ingredients and mix well. Add more matzo meal if mixture looks too moist. Place in a loaf pan and bake in pre-heated 350° oven for 1 hour. Cool slightly, slice and serve with extra horseradish or applesauce. Serves 8.

Meat Loaf

(never fail)

◆

1 tablespoon salad oil
1 large celery stalk, chopped
1 medium-sized onion, chopped
2 pounds ground beef
2 large eggs
2 cups fresh bread crumbs (4 slices wheat bread)
¼ cup milk
2 tablespoons prepared white horseradish
1½ teaspoons salt
Chili sauce
1 tablespoon spicy brown mustard
Parsley sprigs for garnish

About 1½ hours before serving:

1. In 10-inch skillet over medium heat, in hot salad oil, cook celery and onion until tender, about 10 minutes, stirring occasionally.
2. Preheat oven to 375°F. In large bowl, mix ground beef, eggs, bread crumbs, milk, horseradish, mustard, salt, ¼ cup chili sauce, and cooked onion mixture. In 13" by 9" baking dish, shape meat mixture into 10" by 5" loaf, pressing firmly. Bake meat loaf 45 minutes. Serves 8.

Meat Loaf

(onion soup variation)

◆

2 eggs
⅓ cup ketchup
¾ cup warm water
1 package onion soup mix
1½ cups matzo meal
2 pounds ground beef

In a large bowl, beat eggs lightly. Stir in ketchup, warm water, and onion soup mix. Add matzo meal and beef. Mix well. Form into a loaf, bake in greased pan for 1 hour at 350°. Serves 6 to 8.

Meat Loaf

(potato pancake variation)

◆

2 pounds ground beef
2 eggs, slightly beaten
1 3-ounce package potato pancake mix
½ cup water
1 11-ounce can tomato mushroom sauce

Combine all ingredients with ½ cup tomato mushroom sauce. Put into greased 9" x 5" x 3" loaf pan. Top with remaining sauce. Bake at 350° for one hour. Serves 6.

Meat Loaf

(child's play)

◆

    1½ pounds ground beef
    1 egg
    1 teaspoon salt
    ¼ teaspoon pepper
    1 cup bread crumbs
    1 4-ounce can tomato onion sauce

Mix above ingredients together and place in loaf pan.

    Sauce
    1 cup hot water
    2 tablespoons vinegar
    2 tablespoons prepared mustard
    1½ tablespoons brown sugar

Mix ingredients together and pour over top of meat loaf.
    Bake at 350° for 1 hour, basting every 15 minutes with sauce.

Sweet and Sour Meat Balls

◆

1 pound ground beef
1 egg
¼ cup bread crumbs
1 large onion
3 tablespoons fat
2 tablespoons flour
1 cup water
Juice of ½ lemon
1 heaping tablespoon raisins
2 heaping tablespoons sugar

Mix meat, egg, and crumbs and form into balls. Put layer of sliced onions in pot with fat. Place meat balls on top, cover tightly, and simmer on low fire ½ hour. Remove cover, increase heat, and stir until onions have disappeared. Dust with flour, add water, sugar, juice of lemon, raisins. Bring to a boil, reduce heat and allow to cook uncovered until gravy is right consistency.

THE ART OF THE DILL

Parsley, sage, rosemary, and thyme are all very well and most assuredly have their places of honor on my spice rack. But for me, the magical herb is dill. Usually, dill gets passingly included in general discussions and round-ups of herbs and spices. Not this time!

Gradually over many years of eating, enjoying, and cooking, it has dawned on me that many of my favorite dishes depend on dill for that extra zip of flavor.

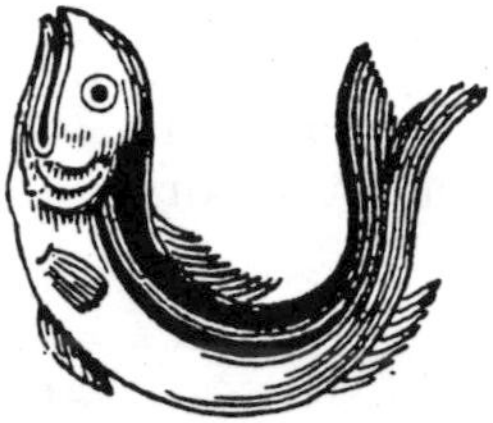

New Potatoes with Dill

◆

1½ pounds tiny new potatoes
3 tablespoons butter or margarine
¼ teaspoon salt
⅛ teaspoon freshly ground pepper
2 teaspoons snipped fresh dill

Scrub potatoes. Remove a narrow strip of peel around the center of each potato, if desired. Melt butter in a large skillet. Add potatoes, salt, and pepper. Cover and cook over medium-low heat for 20 to 25 minutes or until potatoes are tender and lightly browned, shaking the skillet occasionally. With a slotted spoon, remove potatoes to serving dish. Sprinkle with fresh dill and stir to coat. Makes 4 to 5 servings.

Poached Salmon with Dill Sauce

◆

2 pounds skinless salmon fillet or 6 salmon steaks
2 cups water
2 slices lemon
1 slice onion
1 celery top
1 small carrot, halved
½ teaspoon salt
¼ teaspoon peppercorns
⅓ cup finely chopped carrot
¼ cup sliced scallions
2 tablespoons butter or margarine
2 tablespoons potato starch
1 tablespoon fresh snipped dill
    or 1 teaspoon dried dill weed
½ cup cold water
½ cup milk
½ cup dairy sour cream

If using salmon fillet, cut into 6 equal pieces. In a large skillet or fish poacher that will hold the fish in a single layer, combine the 2 cups water, lemon, onion, celery, carrot, salt, and peppercorns. Bring to a boil. Reduce heat, cover and simmer 5 minutes. Carefully add the fish. Return just to boiling, then reduce heat. Cover and simmer until fish is done. Allow 4 to 6 minutes per ½-inch thickness of fish. Remove fish from poaching liquid, cover, and keep warm. Strain liquid, reserving ¾ cup for sauce. Discard vegetables.

Meanwhile, in a saucepan cook chopped carrot and scallions in butter until just tender. In a small bowl combine potato starch and dill. Stir in ½ cup cold water and milk. Add to carrot mixture along with ¾ cup reserved poaching liquid. Cook over medium heat, stirring constantly, until mixture thickens and comes to a boil. Remove from heat. Stir in sour cream. Serve hot with poached fish. Garnish with sliced lemon and fresh dill, if desired. Serves 6.

Cold Salmon with Cucumber-Dill Sauce

◆

6 to 8 salmon steaks (⅔ inch thick each)
1 cup mayonnaise
Fresh parsley sprigs
Fresh dill (optional)
Cucumber-dill sauce (recipe follows)

Place the salmon in a foil-lined baking pan. Spread with a thin layer of mayonnaise and broil for 7 minutes, about 5 inches from the heat. Turn, spread with the remaining mayonnaise, and broil for 7 minutes. Cool. Cover with foil and chill. Garnish with fresh parsley and dill. Serve with cucumber-dill sauce. Serves 6 to 8.

Cucumber-Dill Sauce

◆

1 large cucumber
½ cup plain yogurt
¼ cup mayonnaise
2 teaspoons lemon juice
2 teaspoons grated onion
2 tablespoon minced parsley
½ teaspoon dried dill, or 1 teaspoon fresh
Salt
Freshly ground black pepper

Shred the cucumber; set aside. In bowl, blend yogurt, mayonnaise, lemon juice, onion, parsley and dill. Stir in the cucumber. Season to taste with salt and pepper. Makes about 1½ cups.

Dilled Mushroom Filling for Blintzes or Pita Pockets

◆

8 ounces fresh mushrooms
2 tablespoons buttered or cooking oil
¼ cup chopped onion
¼ cup chopped green pepper
¾ cup dairy sour cream
1 teaspoon potato starch
½ teaspoon snipped fresh dill
¼ teaspoon salt
Dash pepper
Dash garlic powder

Wash and slice mushrooms. Place in a large skillet with butter or cooking oil. Add onion and green pepper. Cook, over medium heat, stirring occasionally, until mushrooms are tender and most of moisture is evaporated. Combine sour cream, potato starch, dill, salt, pepper, and garlic powder. Cook and stir until mixture is very thick. Fill and fry blintzes as per your blintz recipe, or fill pita pockets and warm for 1 minute in a low oven.

40-Minute Potato Soup

♦

1 medium onion, diced
2 large potatoes, diced
1 carrot, diced (use more if desired)
2 stalks celery, diced
1 parsnip, diced
1 tablespoon chicken bouillon or 1 to 2 cubes
1 tablespoon chicken fat or margarine
4 ounces thin noodles, cooked
Chopped parsley
Salt and pepper to taste
Fresh dill

Put all ingredients, except noodles, parsley, salt and pepper, in large pot with lid. Add enough water to cover. Simmer 30 minutes, covered. Then add noodles, parsley, salt and pepper, and simmer 10 minutes more. Snip fresh dill on top of each bowl of soup just as you serve it. Serves 4.

Mushroom and Barley Soup

◆

2 pounds lean flanken
6 marrow bones
2 one-half ounce packages dried mushrooms
½ cup pearl barley, rinsed in strainer with cold water
1 large onion
1 large carrot
1 parsley root and top
6 celery ribs and tops
1 bunch fresh dill
1 pound fresh mushrooms, cleaned and sliced
Salt and pepper

Place flanken, bones, and dried mushrooms in 8-quart pot with barley. Add cold water to within 4 inches of top of pot. Put in onion, carrot, parsley (including top), celery, dill, salt, and pepper. Bring to boil and simmer, covered, for 1½ hours. Remove meat. Take out marrow bones and remove cooked marrow. Place meat and marrow in a blender with the onion, carrot, parsley root, and celery ribs and some of the broth. Blend and set aside. Remove dill from both and discard. Add cleaned and sliced fresh mushrooms to broth with mixture from blender, and cook an additional 20 minutes.

This soup improves with age and should always be made the day before serving and refrigerated, so that fat can be skimmed from top. If freezing soup, let it stand overnight in refrigerator, skim off fat from top, and then freeze. Makes 3 quarts.

Bean Salad with Dill Dressing

◆

1 10-ounce package frozen small lima beans
1 egg
½ teaspoon salt
1¼ teaspoon dill weed
Dash pepper
3 tablespoons lemon juice
½ cup salad oil
1 1-pound can string beans, drained
1 small onion, thinly sliced

Cook and chill lima beans. Break egg into blender and add salt, dill weed, and pepper. Whirl 30 seconds. Add lemon juice; blend. Turn to high speed and pour in oil in a slow steady stream. Mix limas, string beans, and onions with mixture from blender and chill. Marinate several hours. Serves 4–6.

Other Dill-icious Thoughts

◆

Dried dill weed is one of those good things in a small package that can add a subtle new dimension in flavor to the ordinary foods we eat every day.

So add a schmeck, a shake, a sprinkle of dill weed. Try the following:

• three shakes or, if you're measuring, a scant half teaspoon to a 7-ounce can of tuna for salad.

• a sprinkle over sliced tomatoes or in cooked tomato sauces and dishes.

• four shakes or a scant teaspoon stirred into a cup of cottage cheese.

• a sprinkle on buttered (or margarined or cream-cheesed) bread or rolls before toasting in the broiler.

For advanced *dill*etantes, try it in salad dressings, scrambled eggs, and noodle dishes. A friend whose family refused to eat their carrots tried this: She sliced the carrots thin, simmered them in canned chicken soup, reserved the soup for other use, and served the flavorful carrots with a dab of butter and a sprinkling of dill. While her family didn't hoist her on their shoulders in celebration, they did eat their carrots, and one child asked for seconds.

GOTTA PITA POCKET
OR TWO

To me, the pita is not only the best invention since sliced bread but is so far superior in taste and adaptability as to constitute a separate category quite apart from bread.

Pita is neater than bread because it offers a self-carrying case for fillings both hot and cold that can range from snacks and hors d'oeuvres to full-meal combinations of almost every ethnic persuasion. About the only thing you can't serve in a pita is soup, though there's nothing to stop you from enjoying the soup with pita and vice versa. As for "wet" fillings that may cause the pita pocket to spring a leak, there are some simple ways to prevent that disaster (see below).

Once you begin to eata pita, you will suddenly appreciate its wide possibilities for picnics, school lunches, travel and outdoor activities such as hiking and sailing, as well as at-home snacks and meals for family and friends.

While there are several variations available in packages and from middle Eastern bakeries, my personal preference is the smaller size (about five inches in diameter). It's easier to handle and you have a good excuse for eating two.

Great Pita Combinations

◆

- Tuna salad with crisp apple slices
- Chopped egg salad with caviar
- Hamburger with salad and potato chips
- Melted cheese and crisp bacon (Pre-cook the bacon crisp, crumble it with sliced or grated cheese inside the pita pocket. Warm in toaster oven or microwave until cheese melts.)
- Grilled chunks of marinated chicken, beef, or lamb with tahina and salad
- Ratatouille (cold)
- Steamed broccoli, cauliflower, carrots (cold with honey or tahina dressing)
- Cold roast beef with cucumber salad and Dijon mustard
- Cold meat loaf (or meat balls) with salad and dressing
- Chef's salad ingredients chopped small and mixed with salad dressing

Pita Fillings

◆

What you stash in your pita pockets is up to you. Peanut butter and jelly, alfalfa sprouts and tofu, ham and swiss—the choices and combinations are endless. To illustrate the wide range of delicious possibilities, here are 16 suggestions, starting with Falafel, the middle east classic that introduced the pita to most Americans.

Falafel

(fried chickpea balls, tahina sauce, chopped salad)

FOR THE CHICKPEA BALLS
1 cup canned chickpeas
Pinch of salt and pepper
1 cup breadcrumbs
Hot sauce (optional)
1 egg, beaten
1 tablespoon melted shortening
Oil for deep fat frying

Mash the chickpeas. Add salt, pepper, and breadcrumbs and a splash of hot sauce. Mix thoroughly. Add beaten egg and melted shortening. Make small (1 inch) balls. Deep fry until crispy brown. Makes 8 balls.

FOR THE TAHINA SAUCE
A sesame seed paste, tahina is available in cans in supermarkets and health food stores.
   Combine the canned tahina with equal parts lemon juice and water. Add a teaspoon of salt, a tablespoon of chopped parsley and a clove or two of finely chopped garlic. Mix together. Slowly add dribbles of olive oil until you get the consistency of a roquefort salad dressing. (Taste test the first time.)

FOR THE SALAD
Chop up whatever you've got—lettuce, sweet onions, cucumbers—and just a little tomato (otherwise it's too moist).

TO ASSEMBLE
Warm the pita. Carefully cut open the pocket if it isn't pre-cut. Combine chickpea balls and salad. Spoon in just enough tahina to cover but not drown. Makes 4 small pita pockets or two large.

To Prevent "Leaks"

◆

Use dry chopped salad as an interior nest for the main ingredients. Use just enough sauce or dressing to moisten rather than drown. The chopped salad will serve as a blotter.

With moist fillings like tuna salad, line the pita pockets with large iceberg lettuce leaves which function as a kind of plastic lining but are of course edible and crunchy.

Zaziki Dip

(Za-zee-kee)

◆

A romantic interlude on a Greek island left me with a broken heart, a grotesquely peeling sunburn, and a recipe that has since compensated me for those passing discomforts.

Zaziki is both a tease and a temptation to the taste buds. It looks cool and refreshing. It starts off smoothe and creamy in your mouth with just a hint of a tang until it slides down into your throat and chest with a heat bomb explosion of garlic and lemon!

2 medium cucumbers
8-ounce container plain yogurt
4 large cloves fresh garlic
1 fresh lemon
*olive oil (optional)

Peel cucumbers. Cut in half lengthwise. Scoop out the seeds (easy with a spoon) and discard. Chop the cucumbers fine. Combine with yogurt in a bowl. Peel and chop garlic cloves fine. Stir into the mix. Add juice of half a lemon. Stir. Refrigerate covered for an hour or more. Taste and add as much of the remaining half lemon as you like.

Do as the Greeks do. Tear off pita pieces and dip into the zaziki. Or spoon it into the center of a large pita and fold in half as a sandwich.

*In Greece, olive oil appears in most dishes incuding Zaziki. Although a teaspoon of olive oil adds richness and texture, I personally prefer it without oil.

PUCKER FOOD

The famous Peter Piper's peck of pickled peppers surely ranks as one of recorded history's earliest pucker foods. In personal history there come those moments of new experience when childhood preferences for the sweet and the smooth are suddenly challenged by the tart, the tingling, and the tang of the sour.

Peter's peck of peppers was not a morbid pursuit of alliteration or first prize in a tongue twisting contest but rather an exercise in tongue tempting and tasting. As illustrated by the following recipes, pucker foods excite the taste buds, cleanse the palate, and provide poetic enhancement of the sweet.

Aunt Beanie's Marinated Cucumber Salad

(heaven in a jar)

◆

4 large firm cucumbers
1 cup sour cream
2 tablespoons lemon juice
2 tablespoons tarragon vinegar
2 tablespoons sugar
1 small onion, very thinly sliced
Dill weed, dried or fresh

Peel cucumbers and slice into ⅛-inch slices. Place in large bowl of ice water for an hour.

Mix sour cream, lemon juice, vinegar and sugar. Chill. When cucumbers are crisp, drain water thoroughly. Mix with sour cream marinade. Place in large glass jar or jars. Cover tightly and refrigerate. Can be served the same day, but is better a day or two later; keeps for two weeks if it lasts that long. Serve with sprinkling of dried dill or snippets of fresh dill.

Herring Salad

◆

1-pound jar of herring in wine sauce
6 hard boiled eggs
2 medium apples
3 slices white bread, crusts cut off
2 onions
½ cup sour cream
Dash of pepper
Sugar
2 tablespoons cracker meal

Chop herring, eggs, apples, bread, onions together; add wine sauce from herring jar. Add sour cream, pepper, and sugar to taste. Add cracker meal last, to thicken.

Anchovies

◆

Yes, they can be too salty! The trick is to soak them first in cool water or milk for about an hour, and drain and dry on paper towels. Then you're ready to arrange them in strips on roasted pimientos for antipasto or cut them into smaller pieces for salads.

Make an anchovy salad dressing by adding four mashed anchovies to a half cup of creamy Italian dressing.

Make an anchovy pasta sauce by crushing 6 anchovy strips with 6 tablespoons grated Parmesan or Romano cheese and 6 tablespoons of melted butter. Heat and stir just before serving with fresh-cooked pasta.

To add pep to broiled bland fish, whip up some—

Anchovy Butter

◆

Cream until soft ¼ cup butter. Beat in 1 teaspoon anchovy paste or one mashed anchovy, a few drops of lemon juice, a dash of onion powder, and sprinkling of cayenne.

Broil fish. Spoon on a dollop of anchovy butter just before serving.

Sauerkraut

◆

1 quart sauerkraut (from a can, jar, or butcher)
1 large onion, diced
2 tablespoons fat
1 large potato
1 teaspoon caraway seeds
1 tablespoon brown sugar

In large skillet, sauté onions in fat until glossy. Add sauerkraut and sauté five minutes. Grate potato and caraway seeds. Mix. Add enough boiling water to cover. Cook on low heat for 30 minutes. Cover tightly and cook another 30 minutes. Stir in brown sugar at the end.

Scrumptious with brisket, sauerbraten, or old-fashioned Saturday night frankfurters.

Hair-of-the-Dog Sauerkraut Juice

◆

A jolt to the digestive system, this "cocktail" will disperse morning after fog and deal companionably with jet lag loginess. And it is non-alcoholic, so it can only help!

Combine equal parts sauerkraut juice and tomato juice with a half teaspoon prepared white horseradish and a teaspoon of fresh lemon juice. Shake well. Chill or serve over ice.

Add a Little Horseradish

(not just for gefilte fish)

◆

Horseradish clears the head, tickles the tongue, and adds spark to food without adding calories, in itself worth a pucker if not an outright kiss. While you can of course make your own, to me it's not worth the bother when bottled varieties are so delicious and readily available, plain, creamy, or beet red. And anyway, why wreck your mascara when you can just open a jar!

Apart from gefilte fish, consider the following:

For SCRAMBLED EGGS, add a teaspoon white horseradish to 2 eggs.

For MEATLOAF, add a tablespoon plain white horseradish for each pound of meat.

For COLD BEEF OR CHICKEN SANDWICHES, combine 2 tablespoons mayonnaise with 1 teaspoon plain white horseradish to spread on bread.

For BAKED POTATOES, add a dash of plain white horseradish to sour cream or yogurt topping.

For TUNA AND EGG SALADS, add a dash of plain white horseradish when mixing with dressing.

For BLOODY MARY, mix 16 ounces tomato juice or V-8 vegetable cocktail with 1 teaspoon plain white horseradish and a dash of Worcestershire sauce. Add fresh lemon juice and black pepper to taste. Chill. Serves 2. This is a non-alcoholic Virgin Mary; add gin or vodka to taste, if you prefer.

For AVOCADO DIP, scoop avocado flesh from shell into mixing bowl. Mash until smooth. Stir in a little bit of finely chopped onion, a big spash of fresh lemon juice, and some plain white horseradish a little bit at a time while you taste-test for the right amount of zing. Refill the shells and serve with taco chips or pita.

Rhubarb and Strawberries

◆

Cut off leaves and stem ends of rhubarb. Hull strawberries. Wash both in cold water. Cut rhubarb in ½-inch pieces. Combine equal amounts of each in a bowl. Add sugar or substitute to sweeten to taste. Let stand for an hour or so. Taste test for degree of tartness preferred and add more sweetener if necessary. Heat slowly until sweetener is dissolved. Increase the heat slightly and cool until rhubarb is soft. Serve warm or chilled.

Carrot and Green Pepper Relish

◆

½ cup vinegar
2 tablespoons brown sugar
1 tablespoon onion juice
Dash of salt
1 cup shredded raw carrot
½ cup chopped green pepper
3 tablespoons salad oil

Bring vinegar and sugar to a quick boil. Add onion juice and salt. Add to chopped pepper and carrot. Mix well and stir in salad oil as soon as cold. Chill before serving.

Stella Gelman's Cranberry Orange Relish

◆

1 pound fresh cranberries
2 oranges
Orange juice
1¼ cups sugar
Chopped walnuts (optional)

Wash cranberries and oranges. Pour enough orange juice in blender to just cover the blades. Cut up oranges and add a little at a time. Add cranberries a little at a time, until all are ground. Add sugar and let mixture stand overnight. Add walnuts after it has been set. The relish is always better the second day and keeps for weeks.

Beet Relish

◆

2 cups cooked diced beets
1 cup finely cut celery
1 cup shredded cabbage
1 cup lemon juice
3 tablespoons brown sugar
½ teaspoon salt
1 tablespoon each prepared horseradish and salad dressing

Prepare vegetables. In a saucepan, bring lemon juice and brown sugar to a boil. Add the other ingredients and stir well with a wooden spoon. Cover and let stand 5 minutes. Chill before serving.

Cranberry and Apple Relish

◆

3 tart apples, skin included
1 orange, skin included
2 cups canned whole cranberry sauce
1½ cups sugar
⅛ teaspoon salt

Cut apples in halves and remove cores. Remove seeds from orange. Put all fruits through coarse blade of food chopper. Add salt and sugar, mix well, and let stand in refrigerator about half an hour before serving.

Refrigerator Relish

◆

2 cups applesauce
½ cup celery (diced)
½ cup seedless raisins
½ cup crushed pineapple
½ cup prepared horseradish
1 teaspoon cinnamon

No cooking required. Combine ingredients and chill in refrigerator for several hours. Transfer to relish dish and serve with favorite fowl or meat.

GARNISH HELPERS

What exactly is a garnish? Like a lovely cameo on a simple dress, a single rose on a convalescent's tray, a ribbon-tied sprig of dill on a platter of smoked salmon, a garnish is that little something designed to draw attention and give pleasure.

Of course you and the food you serve can get along just fine, thank you, without garnishes. Nor is there a law against serving caviar on a plastic plate. The point is that the enjoyment of food depends on senses other than taste. The smell, touch and appearance are of equal importance.

Garnish contributes color, shape, texture, flavor, and sometimes drama to food. In the words of an anonymous philosopher, it ain't what you do but the way how you do it.

Consider what you can achieve with olives, pimientos, eggs, parsley, watercress, mint leaves, radishes, carrots, fresh peppers, cauliflower, broccoli, water chestnuts, mandarin oranges, almonds, gumdrops, chocolate chips, chocolate kisses, raisins—and a little imagination!

Olives

◆

Black, green, stuffed—as long as they're pitted so you don't break your caps—use them as you would tiles to create designs. Cut pimiento stuffed olives in half crosswise to top a canape or form a circle around bean salad or cottage cheese. Chop black and green together to sprinkle on almost any dish that's bland in color or taste.

For a Sunday brunch, decorate the cream cheese loaf with olives in a design or even the initial of the guest of honor. Dress up tuna, herring, or salmon salad in much the same spirit.

Pimientos

◆

Enhance the creamy brown of chopped liver (chicken or beef) with strips of roasted pimiento straight from the jar. Chop pimiento small and toss on top of an already tossed salad. For a buffet party, serve devilled eggs with an "angelic" smile made with pimiento strips and bits—two small bits for eyes, a skinny strip for the smile.

Hard-Cooked Eggs

◆

Mix chopped hard-cooked egg with parsley flakes and onion powder for zip. Looks and tastes great when tossed on top of a spinach salad.

Chopped egg with onion, anchovy, bacon bits, or sweet pickle is a colorful garnish for a large tomato slice on a cold plate or a grilled tomato slice for a hot dish.

Use an old-fashioned hard-cooked egg slicer to make perfect yellow and white garnish. Arrange artistically on a platter or individual serving dish. Embellish with sprinkling of parsley flakes, dill, chopped olives, or anchovy.

Red Radish Roses and Tulips

◆

Wash red radishes. Cut off the tip and leave only a bit of the stem at the other end. Use a small, sharp knife.

For a rose, make small cuts around the radish in two or three rows depending on size. Alternate the cuts on the rows. Place in ice water. The alternate cuts will stand away from the radish like rose petals.

For a tulip, make 5 or 6 lengthwise slits in the radish starting at the root end and stopping about ¾ of the way to the stem. Place in ice water. When crispy cold, gently slip sharp knife under the radish skin between the slits so that the skin becomes "tulip" petals.

Carrot Curls

◆

Carrot curls are incredibly easy to make. All you need is a carrot and an ordinary vegetable scrapper with a slot. Scrape off the carrot skin. Wash the carrot. Then use the scraper to pare off thin strips of carrots, which will curl all by themselves.

Use to garnish salads, platters, and individual servings.

Combine with fresh parsley, watercress, broccoli, and cauliflower buds to make a "floral" arrangement.

Desserts

◆

Garnish ice cream or puddings with a mixture of instant coffee powder and chopped nuts.

Leftover cookie crumbs and raisins combined look tempting on top of a large layer cake. So does a chocolate kiss in a circle of chocolate chips. Make flower designs from gumdrops, jelly beans, and spearmint leaves (candies or the real thing).

GUILTY LITTLE SECRETS

Everybody has some.

Behind closed doors, hidden from disapproving eyes, even the most disciplined and dedicated will succumb to compelling need. The object of overwhelming desire can range from the shamefully banal to the certifiably tacky with an occasional detour into the truly grotesque.

The following is a confessional of guilty little secrets revealed to me with the understanding of anonymity. My lips are sealed as I pass them on in the spirit of compassion for human frailty and for all who deviate under stress from the things that are good for the body to things that may rot the teeth, clog the pores, dull the hair, or simply look gross.

You may recognize some of these guilty little secrets. You may even share them. Know there is comfort in the awareness that you are not alone.

Frozen Milky Way on a stick.

■

Hot dogs with "the works," chili, relish, onions, mustard.

■

Cold baked beans straight from the can, preferably standing up and in front of the open fridge in the middle of the night.

■

Iceberg lettuce with thick Russian dressing made of equal parts Hellman's mayo and Heinz ketchup plus pickle relish.

■

Chunky peanut butter straight from the jar, preferably eaten with a hooked finger or dull knife for safe licking.

■

Marshmallow fluff by itself, hooked finger or spoon method.

■

Fluffer-Nutter sandwiches composed of marshmallow fluff and peanut butter on white toast.

■

Cold creamed corn straight from the can, preferably while lolling in a bubble bath.

■

Fried Spam and sunnyside-up eggs.

■

Sugar-coated jelly doughnuts.

■

Lime gelatin fruit mold made with canned fruit salad and topped with Cool Whip and maraschino cherries.

■

Rice Krispies and marshmallow squares.

■

The entire serves-four My-T-Fine chocolate pudding eaten at one time.

■

Sliced raw onion and limburger cheese sandwich on pumpernickel.

■

Frozen cheesecake straight from the freezer.

■

Yoo-Hoo chocolate drink on hot or cold cereal instead of milk.

■

"YOU COULD FOOL YOUR GRANDMA!"

Well, okay. Maybe you couldn't *really* fool her completely. But these clever facsimiles of classic dishes are nothing to sniff at. They approximate the look, texture, and taste of certain all-time favorites in a simpler and more health-aware style than the originals.

Taste them. You might like them. Your grandma might like them too.

Uneeda Blintzes

◆

1 pint dry cottage cheese
5 eggs
½ teaspoon salt
1 tablespoon sugar
¼ cup milk
8 Uneeda biscuits
3 tablespoons butter or margarine

Mix the cheese, 1 egg, salt and sugar together in a bowl. Beat the other 4 eggs and milk together in another bowl. Spread ¼ of the cheese mixture between 2 Uneedas to make a "blintz" sandwich. Repeat 3 more times to make 4 all together. Soak the Uneeda blintzes in the egg mixture until softened. Melt butter or margarine in a skillet. Sauté the blintzes until brown on both sides. Serve with jam, sour cream, or applesauce.

White Bread Blintzes

◆

10 slices fresh soft packaged white bread
   (Wonder Bread works best)
8-ounce packaged cream cheese (non-whipped)
½ cup sugar
2 egg yolks

The trick here is to use the soft, fresh, spongey white bread. Cut off the crusts and roll each slice thin with a rolling pin or a clean wine bottle. Each slice should roll out into a pastry oblong similar to regular blintz dough. Mash together the cream cheese, sugar, and egg yolks. Spread mixture on each slice. Dampen your fingers and roll up slices into blintz shapes. Fry in melted butter on medium heat until crisp and brown on both sides. Serve with cinnamon sugar, sour cream, applesauce, or jam. Or, instead of frying, dip them into melted butter and cinnamon sugar mixture and bake in a 350° oven until crisp. Makes 10 blintzes.

Mock Rice Pudding

◆

2⅔ cups small curd cottage cheese
4 eggs, beaten
¼ teaspoon salt
¼ cup sugar
½ teaspoon cinnamon
1 teaspoon vanilla
Nutmeg

Blend cottage cheese, beaten eggs, salt, sugar, cinnamon and vanilla. Pour into shallow 8 × 12 baking pan. Sprinkle with nutmeg. Bake at 325° for 50 minutes or until knife inserted in center comes out clean. Serve chilled. Serves 6.

Mock Gefilte Fish (Canned Salmon)

◆

1 15-ounce can pink salmon
3 eggs
2 or 3 large onions
3 heaping tablespoons matzo meal
1 carrot
1 piece celery
Salt and pepper to taste

Slice onions fine; add salt and pepper. In a saucepan, add water or liquid from salmon to make two cans of liquid. Add carrot and celery. Reserve salmon in another dish. Boil onions, salt, pepper, carrot, and celery, for 10 minutes.

Mince the salmon and bones; add eggs and matzo meal (no additional seasoning). Form into balls. Drop into slowly boiling water. Simmer very slowly (covered) 2 hours.

Serve cold with horseradish, raw carrot curl garnish, and matzos. Makes 4 large, 6 small portions.

Cheeseless Cheesecake

(Zwieback)

4 eggs, separated
1 15-ounce can sweetened condensed milk
⅓ cup lemon juice
1 teaspoon grated lemon rind
1 teaspoon vanilla extract
½ teaspoon nutmeg
⅔ cup zwieback crumbs
2 tablespoons melted butter

Preparation:

1. Beat egg yolks. Add condensed milk and mix well. Add lemon juice and rind, vanilla, and nutmeg. Blend well.
2. Beat egg whites until stiff but not dry. Fold into milk mixture.
3. Combine zwieback crumbs and butter. Sprinkle over bottom of well-buttered pan (8 × 8 × 2) with half the crumbs. Pour mixture into pan and sprinkle with remaining crumbs.
4. Bake at 325° for 30 minutes. Cool for 1 hour with oven door closed.

Cheeseless Cheesecake

(Lady Fingers)

◆

4 eggs
3 lemons
1 15-ounce can condensed milk (sweetened)
2 boxes lady fingers

Separate eggs. Mix 4 yolks with condensed milk and juice of lemons. Beat egg whites until stiff and add to mixture. Line large cake pan with lady fingers. Pour mixture on top. Bake in moderate oven (350°) 10 minutes.

"Friendly Fake Chopped Liver"

◆

1 pound fresh or frozen string beans
1 extra large or 2 medium hard-cooked eggs
1 large onion, chopped
Butter or shortening
Salt and pepper

Boil beans until they are *al dente*. Drain and chop or grind to a fine consistency. Mash egg into the beans. Meantime, lightly brown chopped onion in hot fat, season with salt and pepper and add to bean mixture. Pack tightly into glass or earthenware container, cover, and chill in refrigerator. If you happen to have chicken fat on hand, a tiny dollop mixed in will add to the chopped liver fantasy.

Serve as an appetizer on lettuce leaves or endive. Garnish with black or green olives.

Serves 6.

JEWISH AMERICAN PRINCESS VS. JEWISH AMERICAN PEASANT

A Cultural Comparison

◆

We can begin by disabusing a base canard* as illustrated by the following:
Q. What does the Jewish American Princess make for dinner?
A. A reservation.**

■

Q. What does the Jewish American Peasant make for dinner?
A. A phone call for Chinese take out.

■

Both J.A.P.s have been maligned by comedians, mothers-in-law, and ex-husbands as being unwilling or unable to cook anything. The facts of course speak for themselves in two contrasting Princess and Peasant cuisines and attitudes, each with its own style, passion, and integrity.

While traditionally being a Princess or a Peasant was decided at birth and the tastes of each were both inbred and conditioned by family and environment, the last decade has seen a crossover trend as women have increasingly made up their own minds about their identity. Many a Princess has traded in her radicchio/endive salad for iceberg lettuce and bottled French and many a Peasant has replaced My-T-Fine chocolate pudding with tiramasu.

*Not a recipe for duck.
**Variation: a phone call to the caterer.

As women from Cleopatra and Elizabeth I to Marilyn, Cher, and Madonna have shown, self-invention is the mother of us all. The Princess and the Peasant have their cake and eat it whether it's a patisserie babka or assorted Dunkin' Donuts.

JEWISH-AMERICAN PRINCESS	JEWISH-AMERICAN PEASANT
Radicchio	Iceberg lettuce
Quenelles	Gefilte fish
Scotch salmon and eggs	Salami and eggs
Quiche	Kugel
Bearnaise Sauce	Canned gravy
Bagel chips	Fresh baked bagels*
Frais du Bois avec crême fraiche	Bananas and sour cream
Oatbran muffins	Twinkies
Sourdough rye	Wonderbread
Cold pasta salad	Cold elbow macaroni salad
Baked brie	Hot Velveeta dip

*Nobody in their right mind eats frozen bagels.

JEWISH-AMERICAN PRINCESS	JEWISH-AMERICAN PEASANT
Alfalfa sprouts	Cabbage slaw
Velouté	Canned cream of chicken soup
Nova Scotia salmon	Belly lox
Macadamia nuts	Peanuts
Danish crispbread	Uneeda biscuits
Sundried tomatoes	Heinz's ketchup
Fauchon moutardes	French's mustard
Fresh Tuna seviche	Canned Tuna mayonnaise salad
Stuffed avocado	Stuffed tomato
Turkey breast on pumpernickel with dijon mustard	Baloney on white with mayo
Kiwi with yogurt and honey	Canned peaches with vanilla ice cream

JEWISH-AMERICAN PRINCESS	JEWISH-AMERICAN PEASANT
Caesar salad with vinaigrette dressing	Chef salad with Thousand Island dressing
Crudités with yogurt dip	Nachos and onion sour cream dip
Cassoulet	Baked beans and franks
Vichysoisse chilled	Canned cream of chicken soup hot
Pot au Crême	Junket
Cheese Soufflé	Dumplings
Capellini Primavera	Frozen macaroni and cheese

CHALLAH GO LIGHTLY

Twist and Shout

◆

When it comes to challah, eggs may be a problem. One of my oldest recipes calls for four eggs, including one for the glaze. There is no way to bake challah without eggs, but you can substitute one of the modified egg mixes like Egg Beaters for the glaze for Challah Go Lightly.

Traditional Challah

◆

8 cups flour
1 tablespoon sugar
2 tablespoons vegetable oil
1 tablespoon salt
2 cups hot water
1 cake compressed yeast
2 eggs
Poppy seeds
Additional egg yolk for glaze

Combine sugar, oil, and salt in large mixing bowl. Add hot water and stir until lukewarm. Meantime dissolve yeast in a little warm water. Add to mix. Beat eggs and add. Stir in flour gradually. Mix and stir until all ingredients are blended. Remove to floured surface and knead until smooth and elastic. Return to large bowl. Brush top with a little oil. Cover with a towel and set in a warm place to rise for about an hour. Knead again briefly. Return to bowl. Cover again and allow to rise to double original bulk. Remove dough to floured surface. Cut into three equal parts and with floured hands roll them into strips 2 inches thicks. Twist these into a braid and place in baking pan. Again cover with a towel and allow to rise until double its bulk. Brush with egg yolk or substitute and sprinkle with poppy seeds. Bake in 400° oven about 15 minutes. Reduce heat to 350° and bake for about 30 minutes or until brown.

Challah French Toast

◆

Caution: if you are limiting eggs, butter, and cream in your diet, don't even read this recipe! It can only be made with these ingredients or not at all.

> Challah bread, day old and cut into 6 1-inch slices
> 4 eggs
> ½ cup heavy cream
> Salt
> 4 tablespoons butter
> ½ teaspoon cinnamon

Beat together eggs, cream, cinnamon, and salt in a wide, shallow bowl. Melt butter in large frying pan. Dip the challah slices one at a time into the egg mixture and fry over low heat, 3 minutes on each side until crispy golden brown. The low heat is important so that the outside doesn't get hard while the inside is not cooked through. Makes 3 servings of 2 slices each. (Or two adults and two children!)

SECRETS OF THE MAVEN

In the olden days The Maven learned the secrets of food preparation from hanging around the kitchen, helping Momma, getting under Grandma's feet, watching and listening as the mysteries and techniques were revealed. Little pitchers had big eyes as well as big ears. What's more the little pitchers were asked to pitch in, shell the peas, peel the potatoes, hull the strawberries, and, as often happened, run to the corner for a needed ingredient.

In today's world, where communication is more phone and FAX than hands on, many basic secrets have not been passed along. Not through reluctance or selfishness on the part of the elders but by default. Or, as Shakespeare's Cassius in *Julius Caesar* observes, "Default, dear Brutus, is not in our stars but in ourselves."

As a tournament bridge champion might say, it's the tricks that make a difference. Here, then, from the deepest recesses of the Yenta Archives is the accumulated wisdom of a quarter century's listening, learning, and asking. Pay attention.

About eggs

- Eggs separate easier when cold.
- You can freeze leftover egg white.
- To make the symbolic Passover seder egg look roasted, boil it in dark tea.
- Egg whites beat stiffer quicker if a pinch of salt is added.
- Avoid that greenish tinged yolk in hard cooked eggs by boiling the water, not the eggs. Cover eggs with cold water in saucepan. Bring water to a boil and instantly remove from the heat. Cover tightly. Let stand 15 minutes. Drain and run cold water over the eggs. Tap each egg with a spoon to crack it and make it easier to peel.
- You can tell if an egg is fresh by dropping it into a bowl of water. A fresh egg sinks; an older one rises to the top.
- To separate an egg, break it in half. Hold the half shell with the yolk upright in one hand while you pour the egg white from the other half shell into a bowl. Tip the yolk into the now empty shell while allowing the whites to slither into the bowl below. Place yolk in a separate bowl.
- To prevent "one bad egg" from spoiling the rest, break each egg separately into a saucer before sliding it into the bowl.
- When combining beaten eggs with a hot mixture, stir the hot mixture into the beaten eggs slowly, with the mixing spoon close to the bottom, in a clockwise direction.
- To enhance a simple salad, chop a hard-cooked egg with dry parsley flakes and a touch of onion powder. Sprinkle the yellow-white-green combo over the salad service bowl as a colorful garnish.
- Never try to wash egg-stained dishes in hot water; it hardens the stain. Soak dishes in cold water for a few minutes instead, and watch them come clean.

About soup

- If soup is too salty, add a raw, sliced potato. Boil for a few minutes. Remove the potato.
- To absorb fat from soup while cooking, place a large lettuce leaf on its surface. When it is thick with fat, remove lettuce leaf carefully. Replace with another lettuce leaf if needed.
- If there's time, refrigerate soup after cooking. Once cold, the fat will congeal on top for easy skimming.
- When freezing soups, leave two inches of room at the top of the container for expansion.
- Garnish cream soups with toasted almonds.
- Top onion soup with onion flavored melba toast rounds.
- Get kids to eat their tomato soup with a handful of popcorn on top.
- Add tarragon to cream of mushroom soup, oregano to cream of tomato.
- Cook vegetables in consommé or bouillon instead of water.

About noodles

- Noodles increase by one third in volume when cooked.
- To prevent "gummy" noodles, put 2 teaspoons of salad oil in the water before cooking.
- When noodles have boiled the required time, run under cold water to stop further cooking.
- If you've cooked too many noodles, store the leftovers unsauced in a tightly closed container in the refrigerator. When ready to serve, toss into boiling water just long enough to heat through, drain and serve with sauce, or continue your recipe.

About vegetables

- To keep green vegetables green, cook them uncovered in a lot of salted water. When the vegetables are done, turn off the heat and add several ice cubes to instantly halt the cooking.
- To prevent fresh mushrooms from turning dark while cooking, wash them first in cool water to which lemon juice has been added. Cut off the stem ends. Do not peel.
- If adding herbs to a recipe, use double the amount of fresh herbs to dry herbs.
- When boiling potatoes, put a few drops of salad oil in the water to prevent a ring around the pot.
- For perfect baked potatoes, grease the skin with salad oil and bake for 1 hour in a preheated 400° oven.

About salads

- To crisp celery, stand it in ice water for a few minutes before serving.
- Make peeling oranges and grapefruits easier by heating them for a few minutes in a hot oven. The skin, including the pesky white membrane, will come off easily.
- If making your own salad dressing from scratch, the basic proportion of vinegar to oil is one part vinegar to two parts oil. (Ideally wine vinegar to olive oil.)
- To prepare clean, crisp lettuce in advance, wash the leaves in cold water. Dry well. Wrap in paper towels (or clean absorbent dish towel). Store in sealed bag in refrigerator until ready to serve.

About pies

- To be sure top crust pies come out brown and glossy, brush the top with milk before baking.

- If your pie contains juicy fruits, prevent leakage by sprinkling un-flavored bread crumbs or crushed lady fingers on the bottom crust to absorb some of the juice.
- Make sure your baked crust is cool before filling.
- To bake a frozen uncooked pie, make several slits in the top crust and give it 20 minutes extra baking time.
- To freeze your baked pies, let them cool to room temperature before wrapping in freezer wrap and storing in the freezer.

About cakes and cookies

- Never use whipped butter, margarine, or cream cheese unless recipe specifically calls for it.
- Before blending, let butter or cream soften for an hour at room tem-perature.
- If recipe calls for sifted flour, sift before measuring.
- When alternating dry and liquid ingredients, always start and end with dry ingredients.
- To see if an old can of baking powder is still good, mix one teaspoon with a half cup of water. If it bubbles, it's okay; if not, throw it out.
- Cutting up dried fruit such as prunes, dates, and apricots is easier if you use scissors, which you dip in hot water as you work.
- To plump up raisins, prune, and currants, soak in hot water for ten minutes. Drain and dry thoroughly.
- To stop raisins and currants from "sinking" to the bottom of a cake, shake them in a bag with flour to coat them ever so lightly.
- If adding nuts or raisins to cake frosting, do it just before spreading to avoid thinning the frosting.
- To spread frosting quickly and evenly, dip the spatula in hot water.
- The best frosting technique is to pile the frosting on top of the cake and from there spread it in all directions across the top of the cake and then down the sides.

About measurements

While "a little of this and a little of that" works with some recipes, it generally depends on the long experience and practiced eye of the cook to work. For us ordinary mortals, exact measurements are basic to success. To this end, your basic kitchen measuring gear should include three things:

1. Kitchen scales.
2. Measuring spoons of all sizes on a ring (a bright color makes them easier to find when you're in a hurry)
3. Measuring cups, heatproof and in two sizes, pint and half-pint, including see-through glass or heavy plastic for partial measures.
   - For dry ingredients, heap the measured spoon and then level it by sliding the edge of a knife across the top.
   - For wet ingredients, use the see-through cup and fill to the line required.
   - For shortening, pack it solidly in cup or spoon and level it with a knife. (For melted shortening, measure it after melting!)
   - For honey or molasses, lightly grease the measuring spoon or cup to prevent sticking.

About chocolate

- To melt it, lightly grease a saucepan or the top of a double boiler. Add the chocolate and melt it over hot water to prevent scorching and sticking.

About cheese

- Hard cheese can be grated in a blender in advance and stored in an airtight container in the refrigerator until needed.
- To slice mozzarella evenly, dip the knife in boiling water between each slice.

About boiled potatoes

- After boiling vigorously for about 45 minutes, pierce with a fork to test doneness.
- Drain, turn heat down to low, return potatoes to dry pot, and shake vigorously over the heat for a minute or so to remove excess moisture.

About reheating pot roast

- Slice it cold.
- Simmer the gravy in a pan until it's very hot and then add the sliced meat.
- Cook just long enough to heat through; longer cooking will toughen it.

Index